GLOBETROTTER

TRAVEL GUIDE

PRAGUE

JACK MESSENGER and
BRIGITTE LEE

NEW
HOLLAND

GLOBETROTTER

TRAVEL GUIDE

*** Highly recommended
** Recommended
* See if you can

First edition published in 1997
by New Holland (Publishers) Ltd.
London • Cape Town • Sydney • Singapore

24 Nutford Place
London W1H 6DQ
United Kingdom

80 McKenzie Street
Cape Town 8001
South Africa

3/2 Aquatic Drive
Frenchs Forest, NSW 2086
Australia

ISBN 1 85368 437 6

Commissioning Editor: Tim Jollands
Managing Editor: Sean Fraser
Editors: Laurence Lemmon-Warde
and Catherine Randall
Picture Researcher: Emily Hedges
Design and DTP: Laurence Lemmon-Warde
Cartographer: Desireé Oosterberg
Compilers/Verifiers: Elaine Fick and Genené Dickson
Reproduction by cmyk prepress
Printed and bound in Hong Kong by South China Printing
Company (1988) Limited

Acknowledgements: The authors would like to
thank the Czech Tourist Centre and Naďa Peciválová
for their help in the preparation of this guide.

Photographic Credits: Life File/Emma Lee, title page,
pages 17, 35, 37 (top and bottom), 39, 43, 76, 77, 86,
88; **Life File/Mike Potter**, page 26; **Life File/Nicola
Sutton**, cover (top right and bottom left), pages 7, 25,
36; **Hutchison Library/Liba Taylor**, page 87; **The
Mansell Collection**, page 12; **Robert Harding Picture
Library (RHPL)**, pages 11, 15, 22, 46, 52, 62, 80, 84;
RHPL/Gavin Hellier, cover (top left), pages 30, 66;
RHPL/Michael Jenner, pages 50 (bottom), 56, 60, 79,
83, 93, 99; **RHPL/Christopher Rennie**, pages 18, 19,
24, 55, 63, 96; **RHPL/Rolf Richardson**, page 109;
RHPL/Phil Robinson, pages 34, 44, 45, 50 (top), 53,
54 (bottom), 70 (top and bottom), 94, 97; **RHPL/
Ellen Rooney**, cover (bottom right), pages 4, 58, 72,
74; **RHPL/Peter Scholey**, pages 13, 33, 51; **RHPL/
Bildagentur Schuster**, page 73; **RHPL/Michael Short**,
pages 10, 40, 65, 68, 89, 100; **RHPL/James Strachan**,
pages 38, 101, 103; **RHPL/Israel Talby**, page 29 (top);
James Strachan, pages 6, 9, 14, 16, 21, 23, 28, 29 (bottom), 54 (top), 67 (bottom), 69, 71, 78, 85 (bottom), 104,
107, 108, 110, 111; **Peter Wilson**, pages 8, 20, 27, 41, 49,
51, 85 (top), 112; **John Wright**, pages 90, 91, 93, 102.

Although every effort has been made to ensure
accuracy of facts, telephone and fax numbers in this
book, the publishers will not be held responsible for
changes that occur at the time of going to press.

Cover photographs:
Top left: *Beautiful Old Town Square is the perfect place
to soak up Prague's historic atmosphere.*
Top right: *Colourful, traditional folk puppets are to be
found at markets all around Prague.*
Bottom left: *Attractive Golden Lane's houses were built
in the 1500s for castle guards.*
Bottom right: *Prague Castle looms behind the famous
Charles Bridge lined with baroque statues.*
Title page: *A view over the city of a hundred spires.*

CONTENTS

1
Introducing Prague

Prague is an outstandingly beautiful city whose architectural splendour embodies a rich history at the heart of Europe. The city offers so much to enjoy, so much to admire and to absorb, it is impossible not to feel astonished and exhilarated.

Visitors soon discover that the geography of the city makes it very easy to explore: much of Prague can be discovered on foot, and for weary pedestrians the city's trams and metro provide an efficient and enjoyable means of getting about. Prague divides naturally into five main areas, in part corresponding to the originally separate towns that grew up along the Vltava River. **Staré Město**, the historic Old Town, is at the centre of the city, and its northern part takes in the culturally fascinating Jewish quarter, Josefov. Across the river from Staré Město lies the Baroque **Malá Strana** (the Lesser Quarter), its winding streets lined with magnificent houses and spectacular palaces. Malá Strana is overlooked by the commanding height of **Hradčany**, Prague's impressive castle and cathedral complex. To the south of the Old Town lies **Nové Město**, the New Town, home to many of the best examples of Art Nouveau and modernist architecture in the city, and the location of Prague's famous Wenceslas Square. At the south-ernmost point of Nové Město is the myth-laden fortress area of **Vyšehrad** where, legend has it, Prague first began. In addition to these central areas, the suburbs of the city contain many other sights and attractions worth seeking out.

TOP ATTRACTIONS

*** Prague Castle: palace complex, views over city.
*** St Vitus' Cathedral: Gothic and Baroque church.
*** Strahov Monastery: elaborately ornamented library, ceiling frescoes.
*** Charles Bridge: medieval bridge, sculptures.
*** Old Town Square: astronomical clock, harmonious architecture.
*** Church of St Nicholas: extravagant Baroque interior.
** St George's Convent: art gallery in historic building.
** Josefov: historic Jewish quarter.
** Wenceslas Square: focal point of the Velvet Revolution.

Opposite: *Prague Castle overlooks the Vltava and medieval Charles Bridge.*

Right: *Prague's many bridges span the Vltava.*
Opposite: *Snow-covered St Nicholas Church.*

THE LAND

Prague, the capital of the Czech Republic, has traditionally been regarded as 'the heart of Europe'. It covers an area of almost 500km² (193 sq miles) in the northwest of the country – in the region of Bohemia – and has a population of around 1,250,000. The city is divided in two by the **Vltava River** (Moldau), which, together with its tributary, the Berounka, helped create some of the Czech Republic's most spectacular countryside – Prague is within easy reach of mountains and hills, lakes and forests. The river is spanned by the capital's 16 bridges and is overlooked by Prague's famous '100 spires' (there are, in fact, many more).

The central areas of the city occupy the relatively flat lands adjacent to the Vltava, which curves sinuously into the northern suburbs. There are five islands in the river to the south of Charles Bridge, and a sixth to the north. The castle and cathedral in **Hradčany**, by virtue of the central outcrop of rock on which they are built, are the architecturally dominant features of Prague city centre, while **Petřín Hill** (also on the west bank of the river) looks out across the city and is one of Prague's most popular open spaces. The city is endowed with numerous parks and gardens, many of which are concealed behind high walls along secretive paths and alleys.

Outlying areas of the city (the most recent additions to Prague) begin to encounter the succession of hills and gorges that comprise much of the Bohemian landscape.

FACT FILE

Geography: the Czech Republic is bordered and landlocked in Central Europe by Austria, Germany, Poland and Slovakia. It covers an area of 78,864km² (30,450 sq miles). Greater Prague in the province of Bohemia covers an area of 500km² (193 sq miles).
Population ● Prague – 1.25 million; Czech Republic – 10.3 million.
Language ● Czech.
Government: ● multiparty democracy, elected president.
Economy ● converted to capitalism in 1989 from communism. Main industries: chemicals, engineering, metallurgy, motor manufacture, tourism (Prague especially).
Religion ● Roman Catholic, small minorities of other Christians (mostly Hussites and Czech Brethren) and Jews.

Climate

On the 50° line of northern latitude, Prague enjoys a continental climate of predominantly hot summers and often bitterly cold winters. The **summer** months (July and August especially) can be very warm indeed, but with occasional lapses into surprisingly chilly spells and heavy showers (so take a sweater and raincoat with you). Café society spills out onto the streets and there is plenty to see and do, but if you really don't enjoy the heat, remember that the crowds of high summer can make things seem even hotter.

Spring and **autumn** are the most comfortable months, especially for walking, when pleasantly warm weather can be interspersed with light rain showers. April is the first month when temperatures are appreciably higher. In spring, also, parks and gardens that were closed for the winter begin to open as flowers come into bloom. The colours of autumn are much in evidence along the Vltava, and there are plenty of warm(ish) days in September and early October.

Winter temperatures often descend to sub-zero levels, so plenty of warm clothing is essential. Intrepid visitors will be rewarded with the unforgettable sight of a Prague snowfall (snow can arrive as early as November), but equally memorable is the rather less welcome smog, which can descend for the day and cause problems for people prone to respiratory illnesses. However, Christmas and Prague are made for one another, when the cultural life of the city is at its height.

PRAGUE	J	F	M	A	M	J	J	A	S	O	N	D
MAX TEMP. °C	0	1	7	12	18	21	22	22	18	12	5	1
MIN TEMP. °C	-5	-4	-1	3	8	11	13	13	9	5	1	-3
MAX TEMP. °F	32	34	45	54	64	70	72	72	64	54	41	34
MIN TEMP. °F	23	25	30	37	46	52	55	55	48	41	34	27
HOURS OF SUN DAILY	2	2.5	5	6	8	8.5	9	8	6	4	2	1
RAINFALL mm	18	18	18	27	48	54	68	55	31	33	20	21
RAINFALL in	0.7	0.7	0.7	1.1	1.9	2.1	2.7	2.2	1.2	1.3	0.8	0.8
DAYS OF RAINFALL	13	11	10	11	13	12	13	12	10	13	12	13

CELEBRATING THE SEASONS

The city's **festivals** and arts programmes are timed to the rhythm of the seasons, starting with the most famous of them all, the **Prague Spring Music Festival**. This extremely popular musical extravaganza includes orchestral concerts in Old Town Square and is accompanied by the colours returning to the flowers in Prague's parks and gardens. The heat of summer brings out the city's street entertainers, while the **International Jazz Festival** is the first sign of autumn's arrival. December sees a pro-liferation of balls and dances, when the winter theatre season is also at its height.

Below: *Prague's rooftops are a study in contrasts.*
Opposite: *Art Nouveau stained-glass window.*

Prague Districts

The central areas of **Staré Město**, **Josefov**, **Malá Strana**, **Hradčany** and **Nové Město** contain most of the sights visitors will wish to see, but the suburbs surrounding the central city also have some distinctive attractions.

Vyšehrad in the south provides an interesting escape from the crowds, with its cemetery providing a more permanent sanctuary for many Czech artists and composers, while the working-class district of **Žižkov** can be located from most parts of the city by means of its enormous television tower (Prague's tallest and least popular building) and Žižkov monument.

Constructed largely in the years between the two world wars, the suburbs of **Dejvice** and **Střešovice** to the west have some of the city's finest examples of modernist housing, and southwest of Dejvice is **White Mountain** (*Bílá hora*), the highest point in Greater Prague and site of the eponymous battle in the Thirty Years War (*see* p. 14). The 19th-century suburb of **Holešovice** in the north contains the **Letná plain** and **Stromovka Park**, together with **Prague Zoo** and the chateau of **Troja**.

It is essential to have an up-to-date map of the city, for since 1989 most of Prague's communist-era street names have been changed (in fact, usually changed back to what they were before World War II). Most people have forgotten the old names.

Navigating your way around the city by means of Prague's postal districts (some of which cover a vast area) is unlikely to be of much use, but in the absence of any other information it might be helpful to remember that postal districts 1, 2 and 3 cover the city centre, while the higher numbers cover outlying areas.

HISTORY IN BRIEF

To say that the history of Prague is the history of Europe is an exaggeration, but it is certainly true that the two are intimately connected. Prague has been one of the arenas in which the larger forces and movements of European history have clashed, coexisted and died, shaping in the process the city as we know it today.

Bohemia – geographical area, kingdom and administrative unit – owes its name to the **Boii**, a Celtic tribe who first settled here in the 5th century BC. Over the next five centuries other tribes and peoples staked a claim in the region, a process hastened by the decline of the Roman empire in the 4th century AD. In the 6th century, **Slavs** settled in Bohemia and became the ancestors of today's Czechs and Slovaks, but in turn became subject to the **Moravian empire** in about 830. The empire took in Slovakia and Bohemia, and thus was the only time until the modern era that Czechs and Slovaks lived under the same ruler.

The Moravians found themselves sandwiched between Germanic tribes to the west and the ambitious Patriarch of Byzantium to the east. Successive Moravian kings allied themselves with one or the other: a swing to

CYRIL AND METHODIUS

The exact history of these two brothers continues to be the subject of discussion and disagreement, but their memories are revered by Czechs, Croats, Serbs and Bulgars. They were born in Salonika in the early 9th century and became known as the apostles of the southern Slavs on account of their missionary work. Their knowledge of the Slavonic language helped them enormously in their preaching, which was very successful. They were, however, plagued with difficulties put in their way by German missionaries resentful of their success. Cyril's pioneering work on the alphabet and translation laid the foundation for Slavonic literature.

Below: *Wenceslas is still a monumental figure in Czech history.*
Opposite: *Winding lanes of shops and houses are typical of Old Town.*

Byzantium brought the great Byzantine saints and scholars **Cyril** and **Methodius** to Moravia, who evangelized the people and devised the Glagolitic alphabet in order to translate the Bible and church liturgies. During their mission the Czechs (as the inhabitants of Bohemia were now called) established a stronghold on the site of Prague Castle, but this did not prevent the destruction of the Moravian empire by the invading Magyars in 907. This was to be a pivotal event in the history of Czech–Slovak relations (it split the two peoples politically for the next thousand years), the Czechs allying themselves with the Franks to the west and the Slovaks becoming subject to the Magyars.

GOOD KING WENCESLAS

The incident described in J. M. Neale's Christmas song *Good King Wenceslas* is entirely imaginary, but the tune is on many people's lips when they hear about the Bohemian prince born in 907. Wenceslas (Václav) was murdered by the supporters of his brother Boleslav after the latter picked a quarrel with him. Wenceslas' promotion of **Christianity** and his conciliatory policy toward his German neighbours had angered many of the nobility (especially Boleslav), some of whom were still semi-pagan. Wenceslas was acclaimed as a martyr and made a saint, even though his death was only incidentally connected with religion.

The Přemyslids

Methodius had baptized the first documented Přemyslid ruler of Prague (Bořivoj) in around 873. Under the **Přemyslid dynasty**, Bohemia looked increasingly to the West, the papacy and the Holy Roman empire. Bohemia in fact became an official part of the empire and its Přemyslid kings were subject to the Emperor. The first written description of Přemyslid Prague dates from 965, while in 973 the city was made a bishopric. Building works included the Monastery of St George in the same year, a Romanesque palace on Castle Hill in the early 12th century, and the first stone bridge across the Vltava in 1172.

The 13th century was good to Přemyslid Prague. In 1212, the **Golden Bull** (formal edict) of the Holy Roman Emperor Frederick II granted the Přemyslid Otakar I and his descendants the title of king of Bohemia. Bohemian territory was extended and Prague benefited from international trade to such an extent that **Staré Město** was built in 1234 to accommodate the merchants who flooded into the city (there was also a great deal of German immigration). The Přemyslid dynasty came to a messy end in the 14th century, when the last ruler died without an heir. The kingdom was plunged into a confusion until 1310, when John of Luxembourg became king. Under the longer reign of his son Charles, Bohemia (and Prague) reached its political and cultural zenith.

From Charles IV to Václav IV

The energy and vision of the new ruler ushered in Prague's **golden age**, particularly so when Charles was elected Holy Roman Emperor in 1348. The city became

EMPEROR CHARLES

Charles was an intelligent and cultivated man who could speak five languages. His mother was Czech and he consequently regarded himself as Bohemian, which could only have endeared him to the populace of Prague. It is impossible not to feel grateful to Charles for his enthusiastic building projects and his mania for collecting. His zest for construction led not only to the **New Town**, but to **St Vitus' Cathedral**, **Charles Bridge**, **Prague University** and scores of churches. Prague benefited from the influx of artists and architects whom Charles encouraged, as well as all the artworks he brought to the city.

OUT OF THE WINDOW

What became known as the **First Defenestration of Prague** occurred in 1419, when some Catholic councillors and the mayor were thrown to their deaths through the upstairs windows of the town hall. The event led to demands for an international crusade against the Hussite Czechs from the **pope** and the **Holy Roman Emperor**, but in the early conflicts of the Hussite Wars the Hussite army of peasants won some incredible victories. The eventual and uneasy end to the wars left unrepaired several political and ideological breaches in Czech society: Catholic–Hussite, German–Czech and lord–serf.

Opposite: *Jan Hus, leader of the Czech Reformation.* **Below:** *One of Prague's great astronomers, Johannes Kepler.*

one of the most important in Europe and the self-styled capital of the empire. Many of Prague's institutional and architectural landmarks were built during Charles' reign, including the whole of **Nové Město**. Most important of all, he presided over a period of peace in central Europe that served to enhance Bohemia's prestige and security.

Václav IV succeeded to the throne but could not match Charles' greatness. Religious divisions in his kingdom mirrored the chaos of the Great Schism (1378–1417), when rival popes set up court in Avignon and Rome. The **Czech Reformation** was centred on Prague and led by **Jan Hus**, who preached in Bethlehem Chapel (in Czech) against the corruption of the clergy. Hus was eventually burned at the stake in 1415 after refusing to renounce his beliefs, an event that led to rioting in the streets of Prague and attempts at reform by the Hussites. Throughout, the whole situation was complicated by issues of nationhood, with the predominantly German clergy resented by the Czechs as much for their origins as for their corruption. Such tensions would arise again and again in Czech history and led to the **Hussite Wars**, which raged on and off between 1419 and 1434.

Interregnum

With disputed elections and rival claims to the crown of Bohemia, plus sporadic renewals of violence, the next 75 years or so saw uncertainty and confusion on a massive scale. In 1485 a degree of religious toleration was achieved under Vladislav II, but in 1526 his son Ludvík was killed in a battle with the Turks and the Habsburg ruler of Austria inherited the crown of Bohemia.

THE PHILOSOPHERS' STONE

John Dee and **Edward Kelley** were two of the army of alchemists employed by rich patrons all over Europe. The supreme quest of their alchemy was the search for the Philosophers' Stone, a substance supposed to possess the power of changing other metals into pure gold or silver. The quest involved chemical processes and semi-occult practices and the painstaking analysis of ancient texts for the secret, often thought to have been discovered already by past masters of the art but concealed by them in code for brilliant minds to discover. Quackery, charlatanism and some good science ensued.

The Habsburg Dynasty

Ferdinand I was a Roman Catholic who encouraged the growth of the faith by inviting Jesuit missionaries into Bohemia and by persecuting and executing key members of the Protestant nobility. His successor in 1576 was **Emperor Rudolf II**, whose political skills were limited but whose love of learning and of Prague was immense. He granted religious liberty to Bohemia (angering the Jesuits) and promoted Prague above Vienna as his seat of power, bringing to it the astronomers **Tycho Brahe** and **Johannes Kepler** and the alchemists **John Dee** and **Edward Kelley**.

By the early 1600s, however, Rudolf's congenital melancholia was descending into madness, and he was still without an heir. In 1611, he was forced to abdicate in favour of his brother Matthias (equally heirless, but ardently Roman Catholic), who later proposed that his cousin **Ferdinand II** inherit the crown and continue the Habsburg line. The snubbed Protestant nobility found this too much to bear and the series of conflicts now known as the **Thirty Years War** commenced.

ROYAL STARGAZERS

Tycho Brahe's mass of accurate observational data (inspired as much by astrology as astronomy) formed the basis for **Kepler's** work, from which he derived his three laws of planetary motion. Kepler came to Prague at the age of 28 and did all his most productive work there. His three laws established that the planets moved in ellipses rather than circles, that they did not travel at a uniform speed and that the time they took to orbit increased in proportion to their average distance from the sun. Thus did he convert Copernicus's general description of the heavens into a precise mathematical formula.

Opposite: *A contemporary engraving shows the splendour and wealth of imperial Prague.*
Below: *Count Albrecht von Wallenstein plotted against the Emperor and was assassinated in 1634.*

The Second Defenestration of Prague

Prague's Second Defenestration sparked off the war in May 1618. Two Catholic envoys were thrown from the windows of Hradčany, although this time the victims survived by landing on a dung heap. However, the Jesuits were expelled by the Bohemian insurgents and the **'Winter King'** Frederick of the Palatinate was elected to the throne. Bohemia's independence was to be shortlived, for in 1620 at the **Battle of the White Mountain** (*Bílá hora*) the Czechs were completely defeated by a Catholic army. Frederick managed to escape on horseback, but many Protestant nobles were executed and the heads of 10 were gruesomely displayed (for 12 years) on Charles Bridge. From 1638 the Protestant Swedes joined the Czechs against the imperial Catholics, but it was not until 1648 that the final battle was fought. It took place in Prague, when the Swedes were held off from Staré Město at the Charles Bridge by the city's Jews and Catholic students.

The **Peace of Westphalia** concluded the war, which left Bohemia devastated: the majority of its towns and villages were destroyed, its nobility exiled and their lands confiscated by Catholic nobles, the educational system handed over to the Jesuits and Protestantism outlawed.

The Age of Autocracy

For almost 300 years the Habsburgs continued to rule their provinces of Bohemia and Moravia from Vienna. The 'Germanization' of the aristocracy intensified and the Czech language was for all official intents and purposes extinguished. Throughout the 17th century the Catholic Jesuits dominated political and cultural life, bringing with them to Prague the architecture of the Counter-Reformation – the **Baroque**.

In the middle years of the 18th century, Empress **Maria Theresa** presided over a ruthlessly bureaucratic regime, but her son **Joseph II** (who ruled for 10 years from 1780) did more than any monarch since Charles IV to bring about peaceful

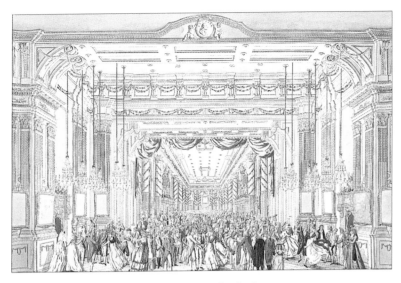

change. He expelled the Jesuits from the empire, dissolved monasteries, overhauled the machinery of government, abolished serfdom and granted equality to Jews. He did, however, retain German as the official language of the empire. It was during his reign that **Mozart** came to Prague.

National Revival

At the beginning of the 19th century, the nascent **Czech revival** of the previous two decades developed into a mature cultural and political movement, but one largely confined to the educated elite. This rebirth of national consciousness was manifested principally in debates and disputes about language, but was galvanized by the work of the historian **František Palacký**, who wrote the first history of the Czechs and who rescued the reputation of Hus and other important Czechs from obscurity.

As the century advanced, Bohemia rapidly industrialized and the resulting rural exodus created for the first time in centuries a Czech-speaking majority in Prague. In 1848 – three years after Prague's first railway was constructed – Palacký presided over a **Pan-Slavic Congress** held on an island in the Vltava.

THE DIVINE MOZART

Individual responses to cities are seldom as strong as those of **Mozart**, who by all accounts loathed his home town of Salzburg but adored Prague. He visited the city five times, on the first occasion early in 1787 to conduct *The Marriage of Figaro*. The opera was greeted so enthusiastically that a charmed Mozart promptly composed his **Prague Symphony** and later in the year returned for the world premiere of *Don Giovanni*, which he dedicated to the 'good people of Prague'. The composer died a pauper in Vienna, but in Prague thousands attended a memorial service for the genius who had loved the city so much.

AMBIGUITIES OF POWER

Edvard Beneš has a mixed reputation in the Czech Republic. In the minds of many he is associated with national hero **Tomáš Masaryk**, and remembered for his campaigning work in the establishment of an independent republic in 1918 and for his government in exile during World War II. Others remember him as a weak leader, too willing to compromise with the Nazis before the war and too willing to do business with communists like Klement Gottwald, the prime minister whom he appointed. A definitive judgement may never be pronounced on this man compromised by power.

National aspirations had begun to divide along ethnic lines, with German-speakers campaigning for unification with Germany rather than for the federalist cause of Palacký and his supporters. Street fighting broke out in Prague as these factions clashed, but Prague's Austrian commander managed to enforce the peace.

Nationalists' hopes were raised in 1867 when a weakened Habsburg empire granted autonomy to Hungary, thus reinventing itself as the Austro-Hungarian Empire. The Czechs were unable to bring enough pressure to bear to gain a similar concession, but were at least spared the fate of their Slovak neighbours, who endured Hungary's policy of enforced Magyarization. Language and ethnicity continued to be volatile issues at all levels of life in Prague: in 1882, the university was divided into Czech and German sections, and conflict could arise over such simple but symbolic objects as Czech shop signs.

World War I and the Republic

When World War I broke out, most Czechs and Slovaks were understandably reluctant to fight on the same side as the Austrians and the Hungarians against Russians and Serbs, and as the fighting dragged on large numbers of them defected to the other side. **Tomáš Masaryk** and **Edvard Beneš** toured Britain, France and the USA to garner support for their version of a postwar division of the Austro-Hungarian Empire, and in October 1918 in Prague the **Czechoslovak Republic** was declared.

In the interwar years the Republic was dominated by the politics of ethnicity: there were still large minorities of Germans in Bohemia and Hungarians in Slovakia, plus tensions between the Czechs and Slovaks themselves. Masaryk was President of the Republic from 1918 to 1935 and it was largely thanks to him that a liberal democracy survived between the wars. His vision of toleration and reform made him a great reformer in the Czech tradition, but in 1935 German separatists won control of the Sudetenland (areas of German population in Bohemia and Moravia), paving the way for Nazi Germany's annexation of same in 1938. Beneš (Masaryk's successor) fled to Britain and set up a government in exile.

Above: *A World War II plaque.*
Opposite: *This column commemorates the 10th anniversary of the founding of Czechoslovakia.*

World War II

The Nazi occupation commenced in 1939 with student protests in Prague and the closure of all higher institutions of learning. The appointment of SS officer **Reinhard Heydrich** as *Reichsprotektor* (governor) in 1941 began an era of severe repression, which led in 1942 to his assassination by the Czech Resistance. Most of the Jewish population of Prague was subsequently deported and perished in death camps. By 1945 the liberation of the city was at hand, with American and Russian troops both within striking distance. The **Prague Uprising** on 5 May 1945 was calculated to provoke the Americans to move in, but in the event the citizens of Prague were obliged to hold out against two German divisions until 8 May, when the Germans surrendered and the Russians took the city on 9 May.

After the 1946 general elections – in which the Communist Party received the largest share of the vote with 40% – **President Beneš** appointed the communist **Klement Gottwald** prime minister of a coalition government. With the end of hostilities, feelings

DEATH OF HEYDRICH

On 27 May 1942 Heydrich was ambushed by Czech agents as he was chauffeured to his office in Hradčany. The first assassin's gun jammed, whereupon Heydrich decided to put up a fight. He was injured by a bomb thrown by a second assassin and in a subsequent exchange of gunfire. He died days later in hospital, in all probability poisoned by some horse-hairs from the stuffing in his car upholstery which had entered his bloodstream as a result of the blast. Nazi retribution was swift and terrible, and the wisdom of the plot continues to be disputed.

had run high against ethnic Germans, and by 1947 some 2.5 million of them had been expelled from the country. Confiscated property was distributed to the remaining population, industries were nationalized and the Communist Party received massive support, both as a result of their postwar policies and because of their role in wartime resistance. After a series of scandals Gottwald was able to engineer a bloodless coup in 1948, effectively beginning the one-party state. Stalin's Soviet Union was the model for the new state, with severe repression of opponents of the regime and constant surveillance by the police.

Although there was still much genuine support for the Communist Party throughout the 1950s, the downward-spiralling economy and the use of fear to quell any protest gradually engendered an organized opposition. A long and complex interplay of popular protest, alternate crackdowns and easing of restrictions by the government, and the refusal of the Soviet Union to support a leadership it disliked, led to the appointment of **Alexander Dubček** as leader and the **Prague Spring**. This attempt at reform was quickly crushed by the Soviets and a hardline regime was installed.

Charter 77 and the Velvet Revolution

Formed in 1977 to monitor human rights abuses within Czechoslovakia, **Charter 77** included the playwright **Václav Havel**, who went on to endure imprisonment along with many of his Charter colleagues. Meanwhile, the Czech economy continued to decline, with falling living standards the cause of further popular protests and resentments. It was, however, the advent of Mikhail

---

THE PRAGUE SPRING

'Socialism with a human face' was the declared aim of the new leadership of **Alexander Dubček**, whose reforms included the abolition of censorship and an ambitious programme of **democratization**. The political and cultural awakening of this Prague Spring of 1968 was destined to be shortlived: in August, the world watched Soviet tanks move in to reimpose communist orthodoxy. Popular protests in Prague were crushed and **Gustáv Husák's** accession to leadership was accompanied by a rigid reassertion of Communist Party control. Dubček was relegated to a minor provincial official until his celebrated return in the revolution of 1989.

HISTORICAL CALENDAR

600–500BC The Celtic Boii settle in Bohemia.
500–599AD Slav immigration.
830 Great Moravian empire.
863–85 Sts Cyril and Methodius evangelize the Slavs and baptize Přemyslid ruler of Prague; Bohemia becomes part of the Holy Roman Empire; The Golden Bull establishes hereditary rule of Bohemia;
1085 Prince Vratislav II crowned Czech King.
13th century German immigration and building of Old Town of Prague; Accession of John of Luxembourg.

1333–78 Golden Age of Charles IV; new buildings in Prague include cathedral and Charles Bridge; Jan Hus preaches reform; First Defenestration of Prague begins Hussite wars; Habsburg dynasty begins with Ferdinand I; Second Defenestration begins the Thirty Years War; Battle of the White Mountain.
1348 Formation of the first university in Central Europe.
1745–80 Rule of Empress Maria Theresa.
1780–90 Joseph II institutes reforms, the height of Germanization;

Separate towns united to form one city of Prague.
1800–1900 Czech Revival and industrial revolution.
1918–38 Czechoslovak Republic formed.
1939–45 Nazi occupation.
1948 Communists gain power.
1968 Prague Spring; An attempt to reform socialism followed by the Soviet invasion.
1989 The 'velvet revolution' and the end of communism.
1993 The dissolution of Czechoslovakia and the formation of the Czech Republic. Václav Havel elected president.

Gorbachev and *perestroika* in the Soviet Union that seriously embarrassed the Czech Communist Party, for the parallels with the Prague Spring were obvious to everyone.

In 1989, the pace of events throughout Europe took most people by surprise. In Prague – just days after the fall of the Berlin Wall – mass protests in **Wenceslas Square** led to the collapse of the government in November and Václav Havel was elected President in December, his anti-communist coalition (Civic Forum) gaining a landslide victory in free elections in June 1990. In 1993, the Czech Republic and Slovakia went their separate ways and the Czechs again elected Havel their President.

The Czech Republic has been the least unsuccessful of the former communist states to convert to capitalism, but it has experienced the same hardships and disillusionments. The country's scenic splendour and the glories of its capital city are invaluable treasures it knows it must guard and protect, for they are the resources on which it will definitely have to rely in the years to come.

Opposite: *Pretty in pink? This Soviet tank used to stand in náměsti Kinských.*
Below: *The Czech Republic's much-loved President Václav Havel.*

LAND OF CONTRASTS

Much of the landscape of Bohemia has been heavily scarred since the end of World War II. **Northern Bohemia's** huge concentration of industries, open-cast mining and lignite-burning power stations have devastated much of the environment, causing its forests severe stress from air pollution and threatening the water table by toxic leakages from untreated chemicals. Its power stations produce the smog that descends on Prague during the winter. Repairing the worst of the damage is essential if the remaining areas of remarkable scenic beauty are to be saved.

Opposite: *The 'real' Budweiser brewery.*
Below: *Prague's trams are the best way of getting about the city.*

GOVERNMENT AND ECONOMY

The champion of the Velvet Revolution, Václav Havel, is the elected President of the Czech Republic but his position is now more ceremonial than powerful. Real power rests with the Prime Minister, Václav Klaus, whose right-wing ODS (Civic Democratic Party) won the most votes in the 1992 elections. Klaus negotiated the so-called Velvet Divorce between the Czech Republic and Slovakia in 1993 and has been the driving force behind the Czech Republic's rapid transition to a free-market economy.

The enormous bureaucracy of the communist regime could not be overhauled quickly enough for most Czechs, but though a start has been made, the country has had to manage its new capitalist economy with the machinery of state socialism. The new economy requires rules and procedures of its own, so for the foreseeable future people are resigned to familiarizing themselves with a bewildering array of new legislation, this time passed and enforced by democratic means.

A Polluting Economy

Confiscated land and buildings have been returned to their former owners, often saddling them with the problems of repair and maintenance resulting

from decades of neglect and abuse. Environmentally, the nation as a whole has suffered widespread damage from heavy industrial pollution and unsustainable depletion of resources. **Greater Prague** suffers air pollution, which harms its people and its historic buildings.

Much needs to be done, but while the

nation's economy depends on such industries as heavy engineering, mineral extraction, forestry and chemicals (most of which have given little thought to the effects of their waste products) it will all take a long time.

Agriculture

Fruit, vegetables and grain are the major arable products, plus hops for the country's famous export beers and grapes for its not-so-famous wines. The once-legendary lack of freshness of most fruit and vegetables on Prague dinnerplates was caused by the country's inadequate storage and distribution infrastructure rather than any inherent problems with its farming techniques.

The Czechs' insatiable appetite for meat (the greatest in the world at about a kilo a day per person) requires intensive livestock farming to satisfy it, with production concentrating on the usual staples of cattle, sheep, pigs and chickens.

Changes

Despite its problems, the Czech Republic has succeeded in attracting a great deal of foreign investment. Prague especially has been transformed by the sudden appearance of advertising and has cultivated an outward-looking, international perspective in its business dealings. The economic transformation has brought social change; the provision of welfare has been curtailed in accordance with the prevailing economic orthodoxy of international financial institutions. People are free to fulfil themselves, but in a social environment that lacks much of the support they need. The Velvet Revolution of 1989 took just days, but the task of evolving a new order will continue indefinitely.

THE PEOPLE

The history of the region has led to a mix of peoples in the Czech Republic. The Czechs make up the vast majority of the population, but there are also Slovaks, Moravians, Silesians, Germans, Romanies (the main victims of any racial prejudice), Hungarians, Poles, Ukrainians, Russians and Ruthenians.

Visitors to Prague used to be struck by the curiosity they aroused in the local residents, even after the years of tourism since 1989. Czechoslovakia was so isolated from most of the rest of the world that its former citizens were still interested in learning about foreigners, their curiosity manifested by much unabashed staring. This has been replaced by a growing insouciance, as the ways of the capitalist world – good and bad – have become familiar.

Conditioned by the years of communist dictator-ship, the Czechs' attitudes to work are taking longer to change. Many people understandably had no incentive to care about and little reason to enjoy what they did in their work. This particular form of alienation can still show itself in standards of service in shops and restau-rants, where the expectations of the more demanding international market may be disappointed. Though such things are gradually dying out, visitors can still meet with a distinctively Czech mixture of casual service and attempts at intimidation.

Below and opposite:
Prague continues to be a city in love with music and dance.

Older Czechs have lost the few comforting certainties of a predictable communist society: pensions are no longer guaran-teed, prices are no longer fixed and the economy is more volatile. Many pensioners feel anxious and confused by the changes. On the other hand, young Czechs have found it easi-er to adjust to the new ways of doing things and are more ready to embrace all things Western.

Language

The Czech language can be dense and impenetrable to even the most ardent Slavophile, with pronunciation causing the most problems. Any attempt – no matter how inept – at speaking the national language will be appreciated, but if it proves impossible the best alternatives are **German** and **English**. Younger people are learning to immerse themselves in international youth culture, the lingua franca of which is English, and are consequently more likely to speak English than German. Staff at hotel receptions and restaurants (particularly those geared to international tourism) are likely to speak English if politely requested.

There are also English-language newspapers, of which the *Prague Post* is the best and most widely available.

Religion

The Habsburg dynasty promoted Catholicism with great ardour during the Counter-Reformation. It is no surprise, then, that most churchgoers in the capital and the nation are still Roman Catholic. Taken together, the number of adherents of the remaining Protestant sects comprise about a fifth of the Catholic total, with the Hussites as the largest single Protestant Church. There is also a small Orthodox Church. Since World War II, the Jewish population of Prague has been sadly depleted, but worship is still conducted at the Old-New Synagogue in Josefov (Orthodox) and at the Jubilee Synagogue in New Town (Reformed).

SPEAKING THE LANGUAGE

Any attempt by foreigners to speak the Czech language will be greatly appreciated. It is a particularly difficult language to master, but here are a few guides as to the pronunciation of some of the trickier letters: the stress in Czech should always be placed on the first syllable.

c like **ts** in coa**ts**
ch like **ch** in lo**ch**
č like **ch** in **ch**urch
ě like **ye** in **ye**s
ñ like **n** in **n**euter
ř like **rs** in Per**s**ian
š like **sh** in **sh**oot
ť like **ty** in no**t ye**t
ž like **s** in plea**s**ure

CZECH THAT ENGLISH

The Czech language is a complicated one for speakers of English to learn, but they should know two Czech words already. 'Pistol' derives from the Czech '*pistole*': over the centuries, Bohemia has witnessed so much strife that it has spurred the development of military technologies like the hand-gun. The other familiar word is 'robot', coined by playwright, novelist and travel writer **Karel Capek**. In 1920 he became known throughout Europe for a play that showed the destructive forces beneath European life and culture. The play was called *R.U.R.*, the initials standing for 'Rossum's Universal Robots'.

Above: *The breathtaking St Vitus' Cathedral.*

THE ROMANESQUE

There are few remaining visible examples of Prague's early-medieval form of solid architecture, most of it having been buried and built upon by later generations to escape the periodic flooding of the Vltava. For this reason, those which can be seen usually take the form of cellars and basements in Old Town, where they are often used for restaurants and cafés. Among the best non-subterranean Romanesque buildings are **St George's Basilica** in Hradčany (the best Romanesque church in Prague) and **St Martin's Rotunda** in Vyšehrad. For admirers of underground Romanesque, the crypt of the cathedral also has some remains.

Architecture

Prague's most obvious and certainly greatest historical legacy is its architecture, which spans the major movements of the last 1000 years.

The architectural style that predominated throughout western Europe from the 13th to the 16th century is called **Gothic**. Parler's **St Vitus' Cathedral** is a supreme example of the style, which is epitomized by ribbed vaulting supporting enormously high roofs, large stained-glass windows with thin stone tracery, pointed arches and flying buttresses. Neo-Gothic (as in the newer parts of the cathedral) is a later use or adaptation of the style.

As Gothic waned in the 16th century it was partially supplanted by **Renaissance** architecture developed from Italian models. Based ultimately on the rediscovery and reinterpretation of the architecture and designs of classical Greece and Rome, it never really took hold in Prague. A superb example of Bohemian Renaissance is the **Belvedere** in Hradčany.

The Catholic Counter-Reformation inaugurated the **Baroque** – a new church architecture in the late 16th and 17th centuries. Its splendour was intended to awe and to reclaim Christians lost to the Protestants. The **Church of St Nicholas** in the Lesser Quarter is Prague's finest example: its dramatic frescoed dome, flamboyant sculpture, rich materials and sheer scale are magnificent. Baroque design ceased to adhere to the Renaissance ideal of serenity: the best Baroque (and there is plenty in Prague) appeals to the senses and stirs the emotions with its psychological depth. No wonder that it was also used for civic buildings and private palaces.

The 19th century was a time of architectural Neo's: Neo-Gothic, Neo-Classical and Neo-Baroque design was used in the restoration and extension of existing buildings – as in the Neo-Gothic completion of the cathedral – and in new buildings as an expression of the Czech National Revival, such as the Neo-Classical **National Theatre**. Towards the end of the 19th century, the **Art Nouveau** style developed: elaborate decoration based on floral motifs and a stylized realism using industrial processes and new materials typified the movement. Its best example is the stunning **Municipal House** in New Town. Before World War I, the Czechs were unique in developing **Cubist** architecture – a style developed from the principles established in the Cubist paintings of Picasso and Braque. The best examples can be seen in the **Cubist villas** of **Vyšehrad**.

Today, Prague continues its architectural experimentation in such buildings as the postmodernist 'Fred and Ginger' project in New Town.

> ### INVISIBLE ACTING
>
> **Laterna Magika** is the most popular of the black theatre companies of Prague. This form of drama originated in the late 1950s and has since won for itself an increasingly devoted following. Its imaginative use of multiple-screen slide and film projection, dramatic use of light, and 'invisible' actors dressed entirely in black, delights the packed audiences of tourists at whom the performances are now chiefly aimed. Prague's traditional folk puppetry also remains extremely popular (you don't need to understand the language). A recent innovation has brought in 'live' actors to share the stage with their inanimate colleagues.

Drama

As you would expect from the nation that elected a playwright to the presidency, Prague has a rich tradition in theatrical performance, which dates from the 1600s (although the city's first purpose-built theatre was only constructed in the late 1700s). Today's popular mainstream theatres may offer simultaneous transmission of a variety of languages and (especially during the summer months) present a considerable number of English-language performances.

Below: *Prague's traditional folk puppets are displayed on market stalls all around the city.*

Right: *Musicians of all ages and abilities gather on Charles Bridge to entertain the crowds.*

Music

Bohemia gave the world Dvořák and Smetana, and Prague took Mozart to its heart. The city's commitment to music is undiminished, and it encompasses everything from classical to contemporary ethnic. Be prepared to wade through the city's extensive listings to find what you want.

Classical music and **opera** are performed throughout the city in concert halls like the **Rudolfinum** (home of the Czech Philharmonic) and the **State Opera**, and in a host of elegant settings such as courtyards, squares, gardens, churches and palaces. The monthly programme is varied and extensive, and is augmented each year from May to June by the **Prague Spring Music Festival**.

Prague's October **Jazz Festival** attracts musicians from around the world, and for the rest of the year the city has a thriving jazz scene in clubs and bars. The same is true for **rock** and **pop**.

Painting

Prague's artworks encompass everything from Romanesque to modernist, with numerous collections assembled and preserved throughout the city. Apart from superb galleries like **St George's Convent**, **St Agnes' Convent** and the **Sternberg Palace**, much of Prague's painting is *in situ*, in frescoed churches like **St Nicholas** or the painted ceilings of the **Strahov Monastery**.

PRAGUE THEATRE

Prague's 'stone theatres' such as the **Vinohrady** stage impressive productions of serious drama, while mime traditions are still very healthy. In the 1960s **fringe theatres** sprang up as popular expressions of theatrical and political dissent (Havel worked in one) and they continue to stage experimental works. Tickets (best bought directly from the relevant box office) for all these sorts of productions are still relatively cheap by western standards.

Literature

The haunting and haunted portrait of **Franz Kafka** adorns T-shirts all over Prague, as the Czechs have come to realize the marketing potential of the renowned novelist whose works were banned by the communists. Kafka towers above the many gifted writers that Prague has produced; his most popular rival is **Jaroslav Hašek**, whose novel *The Good Soldier Svejk* provides a kind of comic parallel to Kafka's work (the bloated and moustached face of Svejk is also all over the city).

Probably the most famous of contemporary Czech writers, **Milan Kundera** has produced works containing overt criticism of the communist state in which he once lived. *The Unbearable Lightness of Being* and *The Book of Laughter and Forgetting* go some way toward describing everyday life under the regime, particularly for intellectuals forced to choose between careers and principles.

Rainer Maria Rilke's reputation has grown steadily since his heyday between the wars in Prague: his short stories and poems are available in anthologies. The absurdist dramas of **Václav Havel** may not be to everyone's taste, but they represent some of the best of the movement that grew up in Prague in the late 1960s.

The **Museum of National Literature** in the Strahov Monastery is devoted to Czech writers. The small **Kafka Museum** is due to be replaced at an unspecified date with a larger complex devoted to the author.

> ### PRAGUE ON FILM
>
> The Czech cinema is not what it once was. Today's film-makers seem content mostly to churn out sub-Hollywood genre pictures, perhaps feeling rather over-burdened by the expectations heaped on them and a heritage that stretches from the silent classics of the 1920s to the New Wave of the 1960s. Lower costs and a tendency to see Prague as a giant out-door filmset have meant that foreign productions have been filmed in the city (most famously *Amadeus*, directed by the Czech Miloš Forman, and the 1990s remake of *The Trial*). Domestic production, however, is in the doldrums.

Left: *A memorial to Franz Kafka, Prague's best-known novelist.*

THAT VEGETARIAN QUEST

As is usual in eastern Europe, non-meat eaters should expect a fair amount of pavement pounding in search of that elusive square meal. The situation in Prague has improved, but Czechs still find it difficult to comprehend that anyone should contemplate giving up meat. For this reason alone, beware the phrase **bez masa** ('without meat') on some menus: it often indicates merely that the main ingredient is not meat – there can still be (recognizable) animal matter in the dish. Czech cuisine is probably best avoided, but *see* p. 116 for some vegetarian restaurants.

Below: *Prague is famous for its pubs and beer halls.*

Food and Drink

The post-1989 influx of visitors to the city has led to an improvement in the quality of food served in Prague's cafés and restaurants and an increase in the variety of cuisines on offer.

Breakfasts vary in size, from simple continental-style meals with bread, jam, tea or coffee, to slap-up hot and cold buffets at the larger hotels.

A traditional Czech **lunch** (*oběd*) or **dinner** (*večeře*) tends to be a straightforward, hearty affair, dominated by no-nonsense slabs of meat (*maso*) accompanied by simple dumplings, potatoes or rice and a sauce/gravy (sauces are uncomplicated and with no strong spices). Meals may commence with vegetable soups (*polévka*) or beef broths with liver dumplings, or appetizers like stuffed eggs, or ham stuffed with cream and horseradish (*plněná šunka*). Otherwise, starters can be little more than a range of cold meats. A selection of bread (*chléb*) accompanies most formal meals and when truly fresh is very good indeed.

Fish and fowl are also favourites: something served everywhere is *Pečená kachna* – roast duck with bacon dumplings and sauerkraut. Carp and trout are the most significant fish in Czech cuisine, with carp being the traditional Christmas treat.

Vegetable accompaniments are often small, while salads are probably best avoided – ingredients are sometimes not very fresh, though this has become less of a problem than it once was.

The ubiquitous dumpling even puts in an appearance in some puddings: in *Ovocné knedlíky*, fruit dumplings (fruits surrounded by a sweet dough) are served with icing sugar and poppy seeds. Strudels are also very popular, as are pancakes (*palačinky*), stuffed with fruit, jam or ice cream.

Traditional Czech **snack foods** are *Chlebíčky* (open sandwiches on sliced baguettes), which can be bought from delicatessens and snack

bars. They come with a range of fillings, often involving smoked fish and cream cheese. Sausages are popular, served either as hot dogs from street stalls or as *klobásy* (speciality sausages) from specialist shops. Street stalls also serve a *bramborák*, a potato pancake served on paper.

The Czechs' consumption of alcohol is among the highest in the world, and Czech **beers** (*pivo*) are justly famous and much copied. They are all excellent and mostly very strong indeed, so if you are new to them, be careful. Opt for draught beer if you have a choice.

Czech **wine** mostly comes from Moravia rather than Bohemia and much of it is reminiscent of German wine. There are some very good **fruit brandies** traditionally reserved for post-prandial drinks: *slivovice* (plum brandy) is the best known (and probably best left alone unless you have time to acquire the taste). *Becherovka* is a herb drink served as a liqueur or chilled as an aperitif.

Above: *Enjoying summer.*
Below: *Simple Czech cuisine, pork and dumplings.*

Coffees are often poor affairs, while **tea** is taken weak and without milk, but the tea bag is served so you can play around with it.

2
Staré Město

Staré Město (Old Town) is the heart of Prague. Its medieval streets are lined with buildings whose façades are emphatically Baroque but whose structures are often much older. Old Town is not an outdoor museum: people live and work here and you may be struck by the incongruity of seeing familiar names of international companies on buildings of fairy-tale beauty. This is also the place where you will find many of the city's best shops, so when you have had your fill of architectural delights you can indulge in some window-shopping. Many of the streets are pedestrianized, making both sight-seeing and shopping more enjoyable.

OLD TOWN SQUARE ***

Old Town Square (*Staroměstské náměstí*) is Prague's finest square and definitely among Europe's most beautiful. Peacefully free of traffic, it may be difficult to imagine it as the focus of violent protest, but in its time it has been the site of several demonstrations, confrontations and executions as well as acting as the city's main marketplace. Today it is the perfect place to soak up the atmosphere of Prague, sitting on the steps of the Hus monument or at one of the many popular cafés which surround the square. In the weeks leading up to Christmas, you can buy delicious hot spiced wine and browse among the wooden stalls that are set up here to sell everything from candles to puppets.

DON'T MISS

*** Charles Street: medieval street lined with superb Renaissance and Baroque houses.
*** Old Town Square: historic square, with Old Town Hall and astronomical clock.
** Church of St James: glorious Baroque interior.
** Clam-Gallas Palace: best Baroque palace in Prague,
** Clementinum: historic Jesuit headquarters, with National Library and Kepler's observatory.
* Týn Church: landmark with ornate spires and tomb of Tycho Brahe.

Opposite: *A view of Old Town Square from the tower of the Old Town Hall.*

MONUMENTAL RESISTANCE

Sculpted by Ladislav Saloun, the **Jan Hus monument** was placed in Old Town Square in 1915 to commemorate the 500th anniversary of Hus's death at the stake. It quickly proved a potent symbol for Prague Czechs. Seeing it immediately as a challenge to the dying Habsburg empire, the **Austrian** authorities in Prague refused to hold an official unveiling ceremony, whereupon the Czechs took matters into their own hands and covered the monument with flowers. The **Nazis** later draped it in swastikas, while in 1968 the Czechs shrouded it in black as a protest against the Russian invasion.

Jan Hus Monument *

Towards the northwest corner of the square is the **Jan Hus monument**. Hus was the leader of the Czech Reformation, protesting against the corruption of the Church more than 100 years before Martin Luther, and has been a national hero since he was burnt at the stake as a heretic in 1415. The Art Nouveau monument completed in 1915 is rather out of keeping with the architectural tone of the square, but a powerful statement nevertheless.

Old Town Hall ***

The Old Town Hall (*Staroměstská radnice*) dates back to 1338, but over the following 600 years it absorbed most of the buildings on the west side of the square. The area of grassland adjoining it indicates that part of the building which was destroyed by the Nazis during the Prague Uprising in the last days of occupation in 1945. (The present Neo-Gothic **oriel tower** and **window** are reconstructions of the 14th-century originals, also

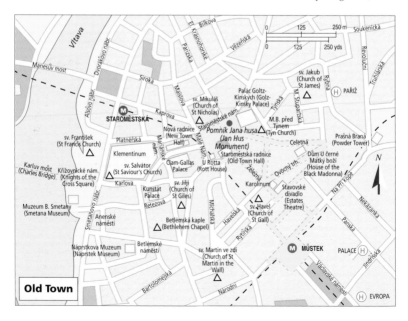

destroyed.) Set into the pavement, 27 crosses commemorate the Protestant martyrs executed here after the Battle of the White Mountain in 1620. The **clock-tower** was added in 1364 (its many turrets added a century later) and its viewing gallery affords superb views out over Prague. The tower wall bears a plaque inscribed with the word 'Dukla': a simple memorial to the thousands of Russian and Czech soldiers who died in the first battle of liberation against the Nazis in 1944.

The hall's beautiful **astronomical clock** was constructed in the late 1400s by **Master Hanuš**. Depending on which legend you prefer, he sabotaged the clock after not being paid for his work, or for being blinded by the town council to prevent him from designing a similar clock for anyone else. Whatever the truth, it was not in proper working order until 1572, when someone managed to repair it. It is surrounded by an intricate Gothic frame and 17th-century niche statuary. Join the crowds that form in front of the clock on the hour to watch the ingenious mechanism at work.

Above: Vanity and Greed are two of the figures on the astronomical clock.

The imposingly Gothic **entrance door** was built in the late 15th century and opens onto an entrance hall decorated with wall mosaics. Next to the door, ornate Renaissance windows incorporate Prague's historic coat of arms, which reads 'Prague, head of the Kingdom'. The **Cock House** on the extreme left of the façade dates from the early 19th century. The Old Town Hall is open to the public Monday 11:00–17:00 and Tuesday–Sunday 09:00–17:00.

Church of St Nicholas ***

Facing the north side of the Old Town Hall, the **Church of St Nicholas** (*sv. Mikuláš*) was built in the 1730s and designed by **Kilian Ignaz Dientzenhofer** at the request of the Benedictine Order. The glorious Baroque façade fronts an interior that has been simplified and somewhat denuded of its original ornament (the church was closed in the repression of the monasteries during the reign of

---

WATCHING THE CLOCK

The skeletal figure of **death** pulls a rope and inverts an hourglass. On the right, the **Turk** (a euphemistic symbol of Lust yet to be renamed) shakes his head, while on the left **Vanity** raises his mirror and **Greed** his moneybags. Windows at the top of the clock open and 11 **apostles** – accompanied by St Paul – process round, led by St Peter. A cock crows and the hour is chimed. The dials show the orbit of the planets around the earth and the sun and moon through the zodiac, plus Old Bohemian, Babylonian and modern time.

Old Town Square

Joseph II in 1781, and was later used as a storehouse). A flawed masterpiece that falls short of its architect's original conception, it is still a lovely church: its curving and intimate interior has a magnificent dome and spectacular chandelier. Concerts are often held here so you can contemplate its beauty while listening to the music of that great fan of Prague, Mozart. Open Tuesday, Wednesday, and Friday 10:00–13:00, Thursday 14:00–17:00. Adjoining the church is **Franz Kafka's** birthplace (Kaprova 5): the gift shop is also a self-styled 'museum'.

Opposite: *Fascinating Old Town Square.*
Below: *Storch House.*

Houses on Old Town Square

The south side of the square has a magnificent parade of houses whose Baroque and Renaissance façades conceal structures of even earlier origin. From left to right, the Neo-Renaissance **Storch House** is a notable exception

to the Baroque façades of its near neighbours. Decorated with a 19th-century fresco of St Wenceslas on horseback, its lovely frontage adjoins that of the **White Unicorn House**, which should really be called the White Ram, as the 16th-century exterior sculpture clearly depicts a one-horned

---

BATTLE OF THE WHITE MOUNTAIN

Fought on a chalk-hill (rather than a mountain) to the west of Prague, this battle in the **Thirty Years War** was between a hopelessly outnumbered **Protestant** Czech force and a **Catholic** army under the command of the Habsburg emperor Ferdinand II. The Czechs were defeated in a couple of hours, after which the Catholic forces looted the city and executed 24 members of the Protestant nobility: these nobles were decapitated, while three commoners were hung, drawn and quartered. The Habsburg–German domination of Bohemia continued until the collapse of the empire 300 years later.

ram rather than a unicorn. The orange house next door is
the **Stone Table**, next to which is the green and white
Poor Wretch's, which still has much of its original
Romanesque barrel vaulting (there is a restaurant on its
ground floor). The next house along – the **Golden
Unicorn** – is where Kafka and his friends attended a
literary salon. The house is separated from the rest of the
parade by the narrow alley of Zelezná, beyond which
other houses to look out for include the Baroque **Red
Fox** (decorated with a golden Madonna) and the **Ox**,
decorated in a corner niche with an 18th-century statue
of St Anthony of Padua. Between this house and its
neighbour (connected by an arch) is the narrow and
atmospheric **Melantrichova Passage**, along which is the
House of the Two Golden Bears (*Dům u dvou Zlatých
Medvědů*). Its marvellous Renaissance entrance portal
(dated 1590) depicts two sturdy bruins amid luxuriant
vegetation. Beyond this delightfully carved door,
designed by **Bonifaz Wohlmut** (also responsible for the
spire of St Vitus' Cathedral), is a well-preserved
16th-century courtyard.

Goltz-Kinský Palace ***

On the east side of the square is the splendid red
decorative stonework of the **Goltz-Kinský Palace** (*palác
Golz-Kinských*). Like the Church of St Nicholas, it was
designed by **Kilian Ignaz Dientzenhofer**, and in the 19th
century Kafka's father owned a shop in its ground floor
(Kafka Jr also studied in the gymnasium on the floors

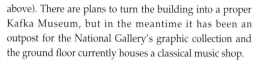

MISSING MEMBERS

Tycho Brahe was a robust Dane whose personality seemed to attract the absurd. His pathological hatred of monks, for example, was caused by a lengthy feud with the Capuchins of the monastery near his home in Hradčany. For most of his life he was without a nose (which he lost in a duel), so he was obliged to wear a selection of artificial organs – including one made from gold, which he wore on Sundays and on special occasions. To cap it all, he died from a burst bladder induced by too much beer at a feast.

above). There are plans to turn the building into a proper Kafka Museum, but in the meantime it has been an outpost for the National Gallery's graphic collection and the ground floor currently houses a classical music shop.

The 14th-century Gothic façade of the adjoining **Stone Bell House** was discovered intact beneath a Baroque shell in the 1980s. The house – complete with chapels and painted ceilings – is used for exhibitions and concerts.

Týn Church *

Týn Church (*Matka boží před Týnem*) is an inspiring 14th-century Gothic edifice whose twin towers and 18 spires dominate Old Town Square and are a Prague landmark. Visible from all over the city, it is actually impossible to gain an unobstructed view of the church due to the houses built right up against it. Until their defeat, the Hussites claimed the church as their own,

but after their overthrow in the 1620s the church reverted to Catholicism, and the gold statue of the Madonna on the gable was formed from the melted-down communion chalice of the Hussite king George of Poděbrady.

A narrow alley off the arcade next to the House of the Stone Bell on Old Town Square leads to the front of the church, but to see the splendid entrance doorway on the north side of the church you'll have to circle round past the rear of the building via Celetná. The door was constructed in 1390 and depicts scenes from Christ's Passion. The chief attraction in the Baroque and Neo-Gothic interior is the marble tomb of court astronomer **Tycho Brahe**, but the 15th-century pulpit is equally interesting. Open Tuesday, Wednesday, and Sunday, 12:30–17:00, Thursday, and Friday 12:30–15:00, Saturday 14:00–18:00.

ALONG CELETNA

One of the oldest streets in Prague, **Celetná** gets its name from a kind of bread baked in the vicinity during the medieval period. The street heads east from Old Town Square, parallelling and intersecting with a warren of lanes and alleys. One exception to the Baroque uniformity of its shops and restaurants is the **Museum of Fine Arts** (*Ceské muzeum Ytvarnných umění*).

Museum of Fine Arts **

The museum inhabits the House of the Black Madonna (*Dům U Cerné Matky boží*), itself built in 1911 as a department store by Cubist architect **Josef Gočár**. Look up to first floor level to see the Black Madonna herself, displayed in a cage on the corner of the building. The building's curving façade wraps round an excellent exhibition space. Inside, the dynamic Cubist staircase and windows are particularly noteworthy. Appropriately enough, the museum has a permanent exhibition devoted to Cubist art – furniture, painting, ceramics and sculpture – plus space for temporary exhibitions. Open Tuesday–Sunday 10:00–18:00.

Opposite: *Dominating Old Town Square is Gothic Týn Church.*
Above: *An interesting market on Celetná.*
Below: *The 15th-century Powder Gate.*

Powder Gate *

The Powder Gate (*Prašná brána*) at the end of Celetná guards the entrance to Old Town. A gate was first erected on this spot in the 11th century: the present one – more a ceremonial tower than a defensive gate – dates from the late 15th century and was given its name after it was used to store gunpowder in the 17th century. Inside, there is a small exhibition on the history of the gate, and access to a viewing platform.

Below: *The splendid Baroque interior of the Church of St James.*

Church of St James **

Along Celetná and north into Templova (strictly speaking outside Staré Město), the Gothic Church of St James (*sv. Jakub*) was founded in 1232 by the Minorites and was remodelled entirely in Baroque style in the late 17th century after being gutted by the great fire of 1689. It has a splendid Baroque organ and more than 20 side chapels. Its chief attraction is the beautiful Baroque **tomb of Count Vratislav of Mitrovice** designed by **Fischer von Erlach**. Legend has it that the unfortunate count was accidentally buried alive.

SOUTH OF OLD TOWN SQUARE

Zelezná heads south from Old Town Square and meets the small square known as the **Fruit Market** (*Ovocný trh*), lined with charming townhouses from the 17th and 18th centuries.

Karolinum *

On the left-hand corner is the **Karolinum**, part of Charles University since its foundation in 1348. Little of this building is as old as it looks, with most of the original construction destroyed by the Nazis in 1945. The university (the majority of whose students were German) became a focus of the Hussite reformists. Hus himself was made chancellor of the university, and he revoked many of the privileges of the German students. This institute of learning, open to all nationalities and using the universal language of Latin, thus became a sectarian divide.

The Karolinum's Neo-Gothic courtyard (reconstructed after World War II), and the oriel bay window (fashioned in the 19th century and based on the 14th-century original) facing the Estates Theatre, are – despite their ersatz antiquity – nevertheless very beautiful.

Estates Theatre **

The **Estates Theatre** (*Stavovské divadlo*) was built in 1783 by Count Nostitz for the benefit of the large German community in this part of the city. It remains one of the finest Neo-Classical buildings in Prague. It was here that **Mozart** held the world premieres of *Don Giovanni* and *La Clemenza di Tito*, and 200 years later it was used for interior shots in the film *Amadeus* (income from which helped the authorities renovate the building to its original splendour). The theatre also staged a light musical comedy in 1834, one of the songs from which ('*Where is my home?*') later became the Czech national anthem. The Estates Theatre remains one of the principal venues for theatre and opera in Prague, with an emphasis, naturally enough, on Mozart.

Above: *The historic Estates Theatre.*

Church of St Gall *

The Church of St Gall (*sv. Havel*) to the west of the theatre dates from the late 13th century. Named after the 7th-century Irish monk and saint, the church (like the theatre) was built to serve the local German community. As with the nearby Church of St James, St Gall's was given the Baroque treatment, its sinuous façade inhabited by a host of sculpted saints modelled by **Ferdinand Brokof**. The rather dark and forbidding interior includes some fine Baroque paintings as well, principally by Czech artist **Karel Skréta**.

Church of St Martin-in-the-Wall

The Church of St Martin-in-the-Wall (*sv. Martin ve zdi*) in Martinská is more of a hotchpotch: a 12th-century Romanesque structure, it was somewhat Gothicized in the 1200s and given a Neo-Renaissance tower early this century. 'Communion in both kinds' (i.e. the taking of both bread and wine by the entire congregation) – one

of the central tenets of the Hussites – was first administered here in 1414, making it a place of great significance for the Hussite Church today.

Bethlehem Square **

Bethlehem Square (*Betlémské náměstí*) is called after the **chapel** of the same name (*Betlémská kaple*) at its northeast corner. The original chapel was the largest in Bohemia when it was constructed in 1391 by Czech reformists who had been denied permission to build a church. Jan Hus regularly preached there. At the Counter-Reformation the chapel was given to the Jesuits, before it was eventually destroyed in the late 18th century. The present chapel – a 20th-century reconstruction of the 14th-century building – incorporates some original outer walls. Open daily 09:00–18:00.

Diagonally opposite the chapel on the western side of the square is the **Náprstek Museum** (*Náprstkovo muzeum*), which was founded by the Czech nationalist **Vojta Náprstek** in the late 19th century in his family's brewery. His collections are now divided between three of Prague's museums, this one housing his international ethnographic exhibits. Open Tuesday–Sunday 09:00–12:00 and 13:00–17:30.

North of the Bethlehem Chapel on Husova is the **Church of St Giles** (*sv. Jiljí*), whose Gothic exterior hides a Baroque interior with frescoes by **Václav Vavřinec Reiner**. On nearby Retězová at number 3 is the **Kunstát House** (*Dům Pánů z Kunštátu a Poděbrad*), the former home of **George of Poděbrady**, a Hussite who became king of Bohemia in 1458. The double-basement of this remarkable house dates from the early medieval period, its later construction simply laid on top, as was the usual practice.

Orders Old and New

Near the Church of St Martin-in-the-Wall is a street named **Bartolomějska**, an appropriately dingy place inhabited by tall buildings that once belonged to the Státní bezpečnost (StB) – the secret police. One of them functioned up until 1989 as their main centre of interrogation. The centre is now owned by Franciscan nuns (who also occupied it before the police took it over). The former prison cells are part of the nuns' 'Pension Unitas', where guests can stay in the cell once occupied by President Havel in the days when he was not so popular with the authorities. Cheap and not cheerful.

TOWARD CHARLES BRIDGE

West of Old Town Square, beyond the Old Town Hall, is the appropriately named **Small Square** (*Malé náměstí*). Most prominent of the buildings here is the **Rott House** (*U Rotta*), a former ironmongery established in 1840 by V. J. Rott, whose name adorns the highly decorated façade. Every available surface of this red house provides the basis for a complex series of paintings depicting agricultural scenes, implements and motifs by the 19th-century Czech artist Mikuláš Aleš. The gable sports the original house sign of three white roses.

Mariánské Square *

North of Small Square, Mariánské Square (*Mariánské náměstí*) is dominated by the **New Town Hall** (*Nová radnice*), built in 1911 on the east side of the square and designed by **Osvald Polívka**. The Art Nouveau sculptures on the main balcony are in stark contrast to the corner statues executed by **Ladislav Saloun**, the self-taught sculptor of the Jan Hus monument in Old Town Square (*see* below). Of Saloun's statues on the New Town Hall, one depicts the famous Rabbi Löw (who cheated Death on many occasions and lived to be 96), being tempted by a naked woman who tries to pry him from his religious studies.

HOW DO YOU SPEAK?

One of the greatest bones of contention between the Czech reformists and the Catholic Church authorities was the **language of worship**: should services and sermons be conducted in Latin (the universal language of learning but not understood by the majority) or in Czech (the language of the people)? The Hussites insisted on Czech, and from 1402 to 1413 Jan Hus preached in Bethlehem Chapel in his native tongue (attracting enormous congregations in the process). For this reason the chapel continues to be an important symbol of Czech national identity, hence its meticulous reconstruction.

Opposite: *Sgraffitoed exterior of the House at the Minute.*
Left: *Jan Hus monument, Old Town Square.*

Opposite: *A number of Baroque buildings comprise the Clementinum complex.*
Below: *The royal coronation route ends at Prague Castle, guarded today by these dashing sentries.*

Clam-Gallas Palace **

Just off the south side of Mariánské Square at Husova 20 is one of Prague's greatest Baroque palaces, the Clam-Gallas (*Clam-Gallasův palác*), designed by **Fischer von Erlach** and built in 1730 for Jan Gallas de Campo, Marshall of Bohemia. The muscular bodies of the giant Hercules (sculpted by **Matthias Braun**) on either side of the magnificent portals appear to writhe and strain under the weight of the entablature they support – a typically exhilarating Baroque device. Further along at No. 23 is Prague's **House of Photography** (*Pražský dům fotografie*), which puts on excellent exhibitions and sells prints of works on display – open daily 11:00–18:00.

South of the palace is the serpentine **Charles Street** (*Karlova*). This was once the main thoroughfare through the medieval town and part of the **coronation route** (*králová cesta*) for monarchs of Bohemia as they made their way to Prague Castle – Ferdinand IV was the last king to be so crowned, in 1836. Lined with Gothic, Renaissance and Baroque façades, the street is still thronged with people, shops and stalls, but the slow progress down this fascinating road is well worth while.

Clementinum **

More than 30 houses and three churches were eventually demolished to make way for the series of buildings that were to become known as the **Clementinum** (*Klementinum*), a former Jesuit college and the largest complex of Baroque buildings in Prague. The Jesuits were invited to the city by Ferdinand I in 1556 in order to win back converts from the heresy of the Hussites. Establishing themselves in the church and monastery of St Clement, they were soon able to rival and then surpass the city's Carolinum (Hussite college),

eventually gaining complete control over Prague's higher education system in 1622. In 1773, the Order was dissolved by the pope and the Jesuits had to leave Prague, whereupon all education was put under state control.

Much of the Clementinum backs on to Charles Street, although there is another entrance on Knights of the Cross Square (*Křižovnické náměstí*), opposite Charles Bridge. There are five imposing courtyards, the first of which contains the entrance to the **Mirrored Chapel** (*Zrcadlová kaple*), all gilt and mirror panels. The excellent acoustics are the reason why so many concerts are held here (the chapel is otherwise seldom open). The **Baroque hall** is near the chapel and is one of the loveliest rooms in Prague, decorated with beautiful frescoes and ancient globes. The leather-bound books are part of the vast collection of the National Library, now located in the Clementinum. The library is open on Monday, Wednesday, Thursday 12:00–18:00, Tuesday, Friday 9:00–15:00, Saturday 09:00–12:00.

The Clementinum **Observatory** is in the heart of the complex. It was here that Johannes Kepler studied the heavens every day in the early 1600s when he was court astronomer (he didn't have far to travel from his

SGRAFFITO

The Renaissance style came to Prague from Italy in the 16th century. It brought with it a passion for sgraffito that continued down the centuries while other styles came and went. Today, some of the most beautiful of the city's buildings are decorated in complex patterns, abstract designs or stylized portraits with bold colours – the **Smetana Museum** and the **Schwarzenberg Palace** are prime examples. The sgraffito process involves the scratching and chipping of a wet layer of plaster to reveal different colours beneath. The direction and nature of the scratching creates the illusion of solid forms.

Below: *The superb riverside location of the Smetana Museum.*

home at no.4 Charles Street). At the top of the observatory is a sculpture of Atlas, while inside there is much in the way of old astronomical equipment to examine – charts and models of the solar system – plus astronomically inspired statues and allegories. Valuable records include the oldest continuous weather reports in Europe, and Bohemia's oldest illuminated manuscript, dated 1086.

KNIGHTS OF THE CROSS SQUARE
St Saviour's Church *

St Saviour's Church (*sv. Salvátor*) is part of the Clementinum complex and adjoins the entrance on Knights of the Cross Square (*Křižovnické náměstí*). Built in 1578, it is the oldest Jesuit church in Bohemia and follows the general plan of the Order's Gesù Church in Rome. The noble façade of Neo-Renaissance and Baroque elements was created and added to throughout the 1600s. The Baroque statuary has become rather dirty, but there is still plenty of it and the whole exterior is lit up spectacularly at night. Inside, some ornamental stucco-work continues the Baroque theme.

Church of St Francis **

Opposite St Saviour's is the domed Church of St Francis (*sv. František*), the official church of the Knights of the Cross with the Red Star. These knights were the gatekeepers of Judith Bridge (named after the wife of Vladislav I), the 12th-century construction that spanned the river in the place now occupied by Charles Bridge. From their

ranks came many of Prague's archbishops. The plan and furnishings of the church make it the only one of its kind in the city – designed by architect **Jean-Baptiste Mathey**, it follows a French rather than an Italian interpretation of Baroque. The interior – extensively furnished in marble – has a magnificent altar guarded by some striking statues of saints sculpted by **Jeremiah Süssner**. Next door, there is a small permanent exhibition of paintings and church treasures, plus a chapel decorated with stalactites.

Above: *A statue of Smetana stands in the garden of the museum devoted to the composer.*

The large bronze **statue of Charles IV** in the centre of the square was erected in 1848 to commemorate the 500th anniversary of the founding of the Carolinum. It depicts an emperor whose absolute authority is leavened with humanity and compassion. Sculpted by the German artist, **Ernst Hähnel**, it's a work that managed to remain unscathed despite the mounting opposition of the Czech national awakening.

From the square, Charles Bridge awaits exploration, but allow some time if you can to explore the waterfront to its left. Facing the river is a splendid Neo-Renaissance sgraffitoed building of golds and greys. Formerly the head office of Prague's water company (believe it or not), it now contains a riverside café, theatre and the first-floor **Smetana Museum** (*Muzeum Bedřicha Smetany*), from which there are good views of the river that so inspired the composer.

BEDRICH SMETANA

Born in 1824, the German-speaking Smetana was a fervent Czech patriot. His life and work were tied up with the nationalist cause: he drew inspiration for his music from the Czech landscape, most famously in his cycle of **symphonic poems** entitled *My Homeland*, and incorporated traditional folk tunes into operas such as *The Bartered Bride* and *Libuše*. His music school was in the **House of the Golden Unicorn** in Old Town Square. A tragic figure, he went deaf at the age of 50 and eventually became insane, dying of syphilis in a mental asylum in 1884.

3
Malá Strana

The **Lesser Quarter** (*Malá Strana*) lies across the river from Old Town and is best reached by means of the Charles Bridge. More than any other area of Prague, the Lesser Quarter is definitively Baroque: a town of houses, palaces and gardens that has remained largely unchanged since the 18th century, its quiet elegance is now the preserve of embassies and consulates from around the world.

CHARLES BRIDGE ★★★
Medieval Charles Bridge throngs with people whatever the season or time of day. It is lined with Baroque statues and is the city's most familiar landmark, affording spectacular views of Prague Castle and the river. First thing in the morning, you'll see street vendors setting up their stalls along the length of the bridge. Most of them specialize in paintings and photographs of the Prague cityscape, but there is also jewellery and other mementoes on offer. Many of these hardy entrepreneurs stand by their posts throughout the winter, fortified by frequent mugs of hot coffee. The occasional busker will ply his or her trade even during a snowfall, but summer is the best time to see and hear all sorts of street entertainers and musicians.

During the hot weather the bridge groans under the weight of thousands of admiring visitors. The view up to the castle is one of the most stunning in Prague, while along the river in both directions there are uninterrupted vistas. Looking southwards, you will see the Vltava's bridges receding into the summer haze, overlooked by the hill of Vyšehrad. Gazing eastwards back toward Old

---

DON'T MISS

★★★ **Charles Bridge:** medieval bridge, Baroque statuary and super views along the Vltava.
★★★ **Church of St Nicholas:** masterpiece of Baroque architecture, breathtaking dome.
★★ **Lesser Quarter Square:** historic, with shops and cafés.
★★ **Nerudova Street:** Renaissance and Baroque houses.
★ **Kampa Island:** charming, peaceful island with park.
★ **Petřín Hill:** panoramic views; funicular railway; observation tower and Hunger Wall.
★ **Wallenstein Palace:** grand palace with superb garden.

Opposite: *The illuminated Church of St Nicholas.*

THE SAINT OF BRIDGES

Europe is replete with bridges adorned with statues of **St John Nepomuk**, mostly in central Europe and the Balkans. The **Charles Bridge** statue is the one that inspired them all, for it was here that St John was tied hand and foot and thrown into the river in 1383. A halo of stars is traditionally assigned to representations of the saint, said originally to have appeared when he entered the water. Killed by the king because he opposed his candidate for abbot, the martyred saint is now entombed in St Vitus' Cathedral.

Town, you'll see a forest of spires and towers. Once you've taken it all in, remember to return to the bridge at night. It's then that the castle and many of the churches are illuminated and Prague takes on a romance and an atmosphere emphatically all its own.

Construction of the bridge began in 1357 at the command of Charles IV, to designs by his court architect **Peter Parler**. The Old Town side has the finest of the two gateways to the bridge, its tower decorated with its original Gothic carving and statuary: St Vitus is shown with Charles IV on his right and Charles' son Václav IV on his left. The vacant western façade of the tower is the result of damage inflicted in the last battle of the Thirty Years War, fought here in 1648. There is a viewing gallery with a lovely vaulted ceiling on the tower's first floor and also access to the roof, both providing superb views of Prague Castle and the Lesser Quarter.

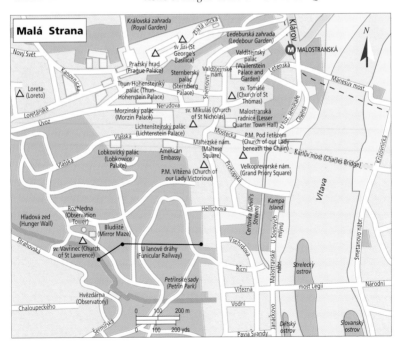

Most of the statues on the bridge were put in place from 1683 to 1714, with the remainder added in the mid-19th century. Much of the sculpture has weathered badly and has been removed to further protect it against acid rain. Those statues removed are being replaced with modern copies.

The famous statue of **St John Nepomuk** was the first to appear, and is the only bronze statue on the bridge, but look out also for **St Vincent Ferrer** and his daunting list of proselytes, and **St Francis Xavier**, raised high by his pagan converts. The larger groupings of figures were among the first to be placed on the bridge: the **Madonna and St Bernard** are accompanied by symbols of Christ's Passion like the dice, the cock and the soldier's gauntlet; while the **Madonna**, **St Dominic** and **St Thomas** are shown with a dog, the emblem of the Dominicans. The large crucifix was for 200 years the only object on the bridge prior to the statues' arrival.

The towers on the Lesser Quarter side are not as well preserved as the others, but the higher of the two can be climbed for a superb view of the bridge and its surroundings. The shorter tower was part of the earlier Judith Bridge swept away by the river.

Above: *Charles Bridge.*

RIVER OF LIFE

Like most major European rivers, the **Vltava** has provided water for drinking, washing and for powering the machines of industrial revolution. It has acted as the city's main sewer and as a trade route. It has often seriously flooded parts of the city. But perhaps more than any of the great rivers of Europe, the Vltava has symbolized the spirit of a nation and of a city, most famously in Smetana's orchestral masterpiece *My Homeland* (*Má vlast*).

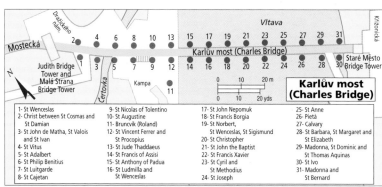

1- St Wenceslas
2- Christ between St Cosmas and St Damian
3- St John de Matha, St Valois and St Ivan
4- St Vitus
5- St Adalbert
6- St Philip Benitius
7- St Luitgarde
8- St Cajetan
9- St Nicolas of Tolentino
10- St Augustine
11- Bruncvik (Roland)
12- St Vincent Ferrer and St Procopius
13- St Jude Thaddaeus
14- St Francis of Assisi
15- St Anthony of Padua
16- St Ludmilla and St Wenceslas
17- St John Nepomuk
18- St Francis Borgia
19- St Norbert, St Wenceslas, St Sigismund
20- St Christopher
21- St John the Baptist
22- St Francis Xavier
23- St Cyril and St Methodius
24- St Joseph
25- St Anne
26- Pietà
27- Calvary
28- St Barbara, St Margaret and St Elizabeth
29- Madonna, St Dominic and St Thomas Aquinas
30- St Ivo
31- Madonna and St Bernard

Above: *Tram 22 stops in Lesser Quarter Square.*
Below: *An angel in the Church of St Nicholas.*

LESSER QUARTER SQUARE **

Charles Bridge leads to the bustling Lesser Quarter Square (*Malostranské náměstí*), which was created originally in the mid-13th century. Principally a large marketplace, the square had its own pillory and gallows in its lower half. As in so much of Prague, basically medieval structures are concealed behind Renaissance and Baroque façades, and many houses have been knocked together to form large palaces. A massive fire in 1541 necessitated much of the rebuilding, while another major event – the cessation of the plague epidemic in 1713 – is commemorated by a column dedicated to the Christian Holy Trinity. In the medieval vaulted arcades still surviving around the perimeter of the square, you will find shops and cafés, making it a good place to stop for a rest before continuing your exploration of the area. The square is divided in two by the former Jesuit college and a magnificent church.

Among the houses and palaces that demand special mention is one on the east side of the square at no. 23, the **Kaiserstein Palace** (*Kaišerštejnský palác*), whose detailed Baroque façade includes four gable statues personifying the seasons. Number 21 on the same side of the square is the former **Lesser Quarter Town Hall** (*Malostranské radnice*), with a Renaissance façade incorporating a distinctive main portal. The **Sternberg Palace** (*Sternberský palác*) at no. 19 on the north side is built where the great fire of 1541 began. Number 18, next door, is the twin-turreted **Smiřický Palace** (*Palác Smiřických*). This green and yellow extravaganza was where the Second Defenestration of Prague was plotted in 1618. Sněmovní, the little road that runs off the square in front of the Smiřický Palace, is the home of the Czech National Assembly.

Liechtenstein Palace *

Taking up the entire west side of the square, the **Liechtenstein Palace** (*Lichtenštejnský palác*) is a combination of five houses whose classical façade was added in the 1790s. It was the home of Karl von Liechtenstein, who pronounced the death sentence on the 27 martyrs executed in Old Town Square in 1620. The palace now holds concerts and art exhibitions. The south side of the square contains vestiges of medieval Prague, with the 16th-century **Golden Lion House** (*U Mecenáše*) at no. 10 retaining its 13th-century cellar.

Church of St Nicholas ***

Dominating the square, the Church of St Nicholas (*sv. Mikuláš*) is without doubt the greatest Baroque church in Prague and the Dientzenhofers' supreme achievement. Commissioned by the Jesuits from their college next door, begun in 1703 and completed in 1761, it is a perfect example of the Baroque ambition to overwhelm the viewer and communicate via the senses an image of the infinite. Christoph, the older Dientzenhofer, was responsible for the general plan and façade of the church, while son Kilian finished the dome and Anselmo Lurago added the belfry, the last part of the church to be built.

The curving west façade of the church, with its harmonious use of statuary, columns and pilasters, is deliberately understated so as to leave one unprepared for the drama of the interior.

Below: *The amazing frescoed dome in the Church of St Nicholas.*

As you enter, imagine the effect such supremely confident architecture would have had on the poor Bohemian peasant of the time. The vast nave is covered in a similarly vast fresco (1500m²/16,150 sq ft) by **Lukas Kracker** depicting the colourful exploits of St Nicholas (a.k.a. Santa Claus). Above the main door, the fabulous **Baroque organ** and case – built in 1746 – was played by Mozart in 1787. The fresco above the organ shows St Cecilia, the patron saint of music. The enormous frescoed dome is 70m (230ft) high and celebrates the Holy Trinity. Powerful statues of the Church Fathers point the way up to the dramatic high altar which is topped by a copper statue of St Nicholas.

Church of St Thomas **

Another Dientzenhofer project lies just off the northeast part of the square in Letenská. The Church of St Thomas (*sv. Tomáše*) was originally a Gothic church finished in 1379. Remaining staunchly Catholic throughout the Hussite period, it fell victim to arson and the elements before Kilian Ignaz Dientzenhofer was called in to remodel it in 1723. Preserving the Gothic ground-plan and spire, Dientzenhofer added an inspiring dome and created a

Opposite: *The superb Wallenstein Gardens.*
Below: *The organ in the Church of St Thomas.*

new façade of extraordinary Baroque audacity, while, inside, Václav Reiner's *trompe-l'oeil* ceiling frescoes, crowded with figures, burst open the nave and dome with breathtaking virtuosity. This light and airy church is definitely one of Prague's most impressive and successful Baroque conversions.

Wallenstein Palace and Gardens ***

North of St Thomas's along Tomásská is Wallenstein Palace (*Valdštejnský palác*), the first Baroque building of its type in Prague and built for **Albrecht von Wallenstein**, military commander in the Thirty Years War. His ambition for the palace was to outdo Prague Castle, and he very nearly succeeded. Dozens of houses and gardens were purchased and then demolished in order for the palace to be constructed, work beginning in 1624 and ending six years later – most of it performed by Italian artists. The impressive interior has more grandeur than glory about it and probably reflects quite accurately the cult of self which Wallenstein seems to have had, as he concerned himself with every last detail of the design.

The double-height main hall is the most memorable room in the palace, with a richly stuccoed ceiling acting as a frame to a fresco portraying Wallenstein as a triumphant Mars riding his chariot. Used mainly for state functions, the hall occasionally hosts public concerts. After Mars, any last pretensions to humility are firmly laid to rest in the garden pavilion, where Wallenstein is depicted as Achilles lording it over assembled gods and sundry heroic mortals. The gardens of the palace are in fact accessible only from Letenská. They include a series of 20th-century copies of some terrific bronze statues by **Adriaen de Vries**, a grotto and ponds with fountains. The palace's riding school is used by the National Gallery for temporary exhibitions.

WALLENSTEIN

Albrecht von Wallenstein (1583–1634) was a member of the Protestant nobility who converted to Catholicism in 1620. Emperor Ferdinand enrolled him as a **mercenary** in the imperial army and Wallenstein won a series of impressive victories, conquering most of Germany and in 1632 defeating the Swedes. Eventually, Wallenstein's secret negotiations with the enemy, plus his highly visible passion for self-aggrandizement, led to his downfall. On the verge of having himself proclaimed king of Bohemia, Wallenstein was **assassinated** in 1634 on the orders of the Emperor. He is the hero of Schiller's dramatic epic *Wallenstein*.

JAN NERUDA

Born in 1834, Neruda was the son of the keeper of the canteen of a military barracks. After a good education, he went on to become a journalist in 1858, soon making his mark as a trenchant literary critic. A writer of prose and poetry, his collection of short stories entitled **Prague Tales** describes the bohemian life he knew in and around Nerudova, while his best collection of poems is entitled **Ballady**. He died in 1891. Pablo Neruda, the Chilean writer, was no relation to Jan but took his pen name from the Czech author he so admired.

Below: *Watch out for the Red Lion and the Three Fiddles on winding Nerudova Street (opposite).*

Ledebour Garden *

Across the road from Wallenstein Palace, the Ledebour Garden (*Ledeburská Zahrada*) on Valdštejnská comprises a series of gorgeous terraced gardens on the slopes beneath Prague Castle, a perfect place to take a break from admiring architecture. Gardens first replaced the terraces of vines on these slopes in the 16th century (when the palace-building boom began), and in the 18th century Baroque statuary and fountains were added. With staircases and balustrades, archways and loggias, the garden possesses a bewitching combination of faded formality and stunning views out over Prague. It must be noted that some of the old staircases are crumbling and are currently being restored to meet safe standards. There is also a beautiful *sala terrena* (pavilion) designed by Giovanni Battista Alliprandi.

Nerudova Street **

Nerudova Street (*Nerudova ulice*) heads upwards toward the castle from the northwest corner of Lesser Quarter Square. It's a steep, narrow road and quite a climb, although the panoramic views at the top are well worth the effort. Historically, this is the place where the city's artists made their home and you will still see craft shops and galleries dotted around, although they are outnumbered these days by cafés and beer halls. The street is named after the writer **Jan Neruda**, who lived in the **House at the Two Suns** (no. 47) in the middle of the 19th century. The house has its own sign with said suns, just one of many similarly interesting signs along Nerudova. Look out for the **Red Eagle** (no. 6), the **Three Fiddles** (no. 12), the **Golden Cup** (no. 16), the **Golden Key** (no. 27), the **Golden Horseshoe** (no. 34), the **Red Lion** (no. 41), **Green Lobster** (no. 43) and the **White Swan** (no. 49).

As well as these houses there are some larger Baroque buildings, two of which stand out. The **Morzin Palace** (*Morzinský palác*) at number 5 is the Romanian embassy. The façade includes a first-floor balcony supported by two beefy Moors (a pun on 'Morzin') sculpted by **Ferdinand Brokof**. In fact, the sculptures are so large they take over the pavement, forcing pedestrians into the street on crowded summer days. The **Thun-Hohenstein Palace** (*Thun-Hohenštejnský palác*) at number 20 – the Italian embassy – can be identified easily by its two eagles sculpted by **Matthias Braun**. The birds definitely look menacing enough, but are too busy holding up the entranceway to pose a serious threat.

Italian Street (*Vlašská ulice*) roughly parallels Nerudova. The street's name refers to the community of Italian artists and craftsmen who once lived here, working on such projects as the castle. The American embassy is based in the former **Italian hospital**, a fine Baroque building with courtyard. The German embassy is in the superb **Lobkowicz Palace** (*Lobkovický palác*), whose splendid garden witnessed a famous invasion of East German crowds in September 1989. Note the different sculpted faces that peer down from the first-floor windows.

> **OVER THE WALL**
>
> In 1989, when the Soviet empire was unravelling and communist dictatorships were tottering, Czechoslovakia was a favoured **escape route** for **East Germans** fleeing their country. Thousands of them made their way to the West German embassy in **Lobkowicz Palace**, demanding the West German citizenship which had always remained their right. The gardens of the palace quickly became a quagmire, as families abandoned their Trabants, climbed into the grounds and camped in makeshift shelters. The embassy's resources were severely stretched before the breach of the **Berlin Wall** brought about the *de facto* reunification of Germany.

KAMPA *

Known as 'Little Venice' – solely because of the narrow canal and former millrace called Devil's Stream (*Certovka*) which separates it from the left bank – Kampa was flooded repeatedly before the Vltava was dammed in the 1950s. The steps up to Charles Bridge were built to provide an exit from the island after many people drowned in one such flood because they had no means of escape. Before the fire of 1541 which swept through Malá Strana, Kampa's banks were also prone to instability, but flotsam created by the destruction of the blaze was used to strengthen the shifting shoreline.

Below: *Kampa Island sits alongside Charles Bridge and provides a peaceful refuge from the rest of the city.*

SOUTHERN MALA STRANA

South of Lesser Quarter Square, between the river and the busy **Karmelitská**, is the delightful **Maltese Square** (*Maltézské náměstí*). **Ferdinand Brokof's** statue of St John the Baptist – sculpted in 1715 – is in the centre of the square, which is named after the Maltese Knights whose priory once stood here. Maltese crosses adorn the square and the knights' church (Our Lady Beneath the Chain) can still be seen nearby.

Continuing from Maltese Square towards the river, you cross over to **Kampa**, the largest island in the river, separated from the Lesser Quarter by a narrow canal and connected to Charles Bridge by flights of steps. There are three watermills on the island, plus a peaceful park and square in which to wander.

Petřín Hill *

On the western flank of the Lesser Quarter, the steep and wooded slope of Petřín Hill climbs to a height of 318m (960ft), providing superb views over Prague and across to the castle and cathedral. The largest green space in Prague, it is popular for walks and picnics, particularly in the spring, when the fruit trees (remnants of the formal gardens which were once here) come into blossom.

You can either ascend the hill by following the winding paths or, if your legs need a rest, take the **funicular railway**, which was built originally for the 1891 Prague Exhibition. Trains depart from the lower station near Ujezd. Disembark at Nebozízek station at the half-way point for a splendid view from the station restaurant.

At the top of the hill are the remains of Prague's **Hunger Wall** (*Hladová zed*),

which ascends the hill from the east and then follows a northwesterly direction toward Strahov Monastery. This was the southernmost part of Prague's old city walls, commissioned by Charles IV and completed in 1362. Known for centuries as the Hunger Wall, the story goes that Charles ordered it to be built in order to provide employment to the poor during a famine.

To the south of the summit station is the **Observatory** (*Hvězdárna*), which provides various fixed telescopes for use by amateur astronomers, and to the north is the **Church of St Lawrence** (*sv. Vavřinec*), built in the 1770s complete with Baroque cupola and onion-domed towers.

Beyond the church are more remnants of the 1891 exhibition, the most prominent of which is another city landmark, the 60m (200ft) **Observation Tower** (*Rozhledna*). Based on the design of the Eiffel Tower in Paris, its top (reached by an interminable spiral staircase) provides panoramic views. Near the tower the crazily distorting mirrors of the **Mirror Maze** (*Zrcadlové bludiště*) provide amusement for visitors of all ages. The maze leads to a diorama depicting the defence of Prague against the Swedes on Charles Bridge in 1648. The maze is open daily, April–October, 09:30–18:30; November–March, Saturday and Sunday, 09:00–16:00.

Above: *This mural tribute to John Lennon can be found in Grand Priory Square, just around the corner from Maltese Square.*

MAKING TRACKS

Prior to 1914, the **funicular railway's** method of propulsion was water. The two trains, each at opposite ends of the line, were equipped with water tanks, which would be emptied at the bottom of the hill and filled at the top – thus, the heavier train at the top would descend, pulling up the lighter train as it did so. After 1914, the line was converted to electricity, but in the 1960s parts of it began to collapse as 19th-century mineworkings began to shift. The hill was shored up, but it took 25 years for the railway to be repaired.

4
Hradčany

The castle (*Hrad*) has been the seat of power in Bohemia since the 9th century, although it has been rebuilt and added to many times since then. The official residence of presidents of the republic, it encloses St Vitus' Cathedral and is itself bordered by the ministries and agencies of government in Hradčany.

PRAGUE CASTLE ***

Less a castle and more a series of apartments, houses, palaces and churches, Prague Castle's austere face gazes down upon the city, conscious of its own power and authority. The two architects principally responsible for the look of the place today are **Nicolo Pacassi** and **Josip Plečník**. Pacassi – architect to Empress Maria Theresa in the 18th century – amalgamated previously separate wings into the Neo-Classical block which presents itself to the city below. Plečník was commissioned in the 1920s to restore and modernize various other wings and apartments, his eclectic style making his contributions distinct and controversial.

First and Second Courtyards

The castle entrance is guarded by huge copies of the dramatically poised **fighting giants** sculpted by **Ignaz Plazer** in the 18th century. The human guards of the castle nowadays are the presidential sentries, in their smart blue uniforms designed by the costume designer of the film *Amadeus*, at President Havel's request. At noon each day, the changing of the guard is accompanied

DON'T MISS

*** **Castle Square:**
palace-lined square.
*** **Prague Castle:** churches,
galleries, palaces and gardens.
*** **St Vitus' Cathedral:**
chapel of St Wenceslas;
Habsburg Mausoleum.
*** **Sternberg Palace:**
National Gallery collection.
** **Belvedere:** Renaissance
palace and exhibition centre.
** **Strahov Monastery:** 800-
year-old library collection,
beautiful church and gardens.
* **Loreto Chapel:** historic
place of pilgrimage.

Opposite: *A view of Prague Castle and St Vitus' Cathedral.*

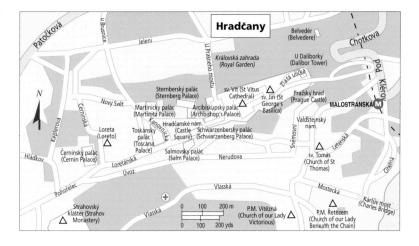

Hradčany

Patočkova · U Brusnice · Jeleni · Belvedér (Belvedere) · Chotkova

U Prašného mostu · Královská zahrada (Royal Garden) · U Daliborky (Dalibor Tower) · pod Kletov

Zlatá ulička

Sternberský palác (Sternberg Palace) · sv. Vít (St Vitus Cathedral) · sv. Jiří (St George's Basilica) · Pražský hrad (Prague Castle) · MALOSTRANSKÁ Ⓜ

Nový Svět · Martinický palác (Martinitz Palace) · Arcibiskupský palác (Archbishop's Palace)

Keplerova · Černínská · Loreta (Loreto) · Toskánský palác (Toscana Palace) · Hradčanské nám. (Castle Square) · Schwarzenbersky palác (Schwarzenberg Palace) · Valdštejnský nám. · Šternovní · Letenská

Hládkov · Černínský palác (Cernin Palace) · Loretánská · Salmovský palác (Salm Palace) · Neruḋova · sv. Tomáš (Church of St Thomas) · Chaha

Úvoz · Vlašská · Mostecká · Karlův most (Charles Bridge)

Pohořelec · Strahovský klášter (Strahov Monastery) · Vlašská · P.M. Vítězná (Church of our Lady Victorious) · P.M. Řetězem (Church of our Lady Beneath the Chain)

0   100   200 m
0   100   200 yds

by a brass band which appears rather unexpectedly at the first floor windows of the courtyard and plays a catchy modern fanfare. Once safely past them and into the first courtyard, another beautiful gate awaits you.

The **Matthias Gate** was originally a free-standing arch when first erected in 1614, but it was later incorporated into Pacassi's new façade, with the addition of monumental staircases on each side which lead to the north and south wings of the castle. In the south wing there are the presidential apartments (unfortunately not open to the public), while the north wing contains the glittering **Spanish Hall**. This magnificent white and gold room is lined with mirrors and hung with chandeliers, and is surely one of the most beautiful in Europe. It was splendidly decorated for the coronation of Franz Josef I in 1705, but the monarch failed to turn up. Thereafter the room was not used until 1836, when the mirrors were added for the coronation of Ferdinand V. Consult concert listings while you are in Prague: you may be lucky enough to see the hall.

The second courtyard is dominated by enclosing façades overlooked by the spires of St Vitus, while on the right is the little 18th-century **Church of the Holy Cross**, now an information and ticket office. A single ticket bought here will gain you entry to the cathedral, St George's Basilica, the Powder Tower and the Royal Palace.

Picture Gallery **

Opposite the church are the royal stables, which were renovated in the mid-1960s and now house the castle's art collection (*Obrazárna Pražského hradu*). Emperor Rudolf II's collection was plundered extensively by the Swedes in 1648, and the National Gallery has most of the rest, but what remains here is well worth seeing. Most of the artworks were produced in the 16th to 18th centuries and among them is a sculpted portrait of Rudolf himself by **Adriaen de Vries**. The renovations of the stables also revealed what remains of the **Church of Our Lady**, thought to have been built in the 9th century when the Přemyslid dynasty was Christianized.

St Vitus' Cathedral ***

The enormous Gothic pile of the cathedral (the largest in the Czech Republic) takes up most of the third courtyard of the castle. The building owes its existence to Charles IV, who commissioned its first architect in the 1340s: neither would have reckoned on the work continuing on

> **PETER PARLER**
>
> Charles IV's court architect was a Swabian German, born in 1330. Parler (just 23 years old) and his workshop team took over responsibility for the cathedral in 1352 and to them can safely be attributed the sculpted triforium, the choir and the south tower. The splendid **Golden Gate** with its delicate supporting ribs and the **Chapel of St Wenceslas** are solely Parler's work. He blazed the trail toward realism in sculpture and his mastery of vaulting was unsurpassed: both were tremendously influential on the art and architecture that followed. With his employer's patronage, he made his mark all over Prague.

Opposite: *Soldiers stand guard at strategic locations around Prague's cathedral and castle buildings.*

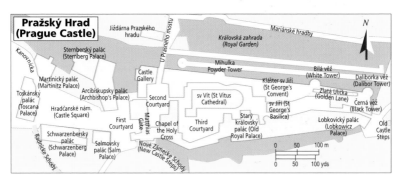

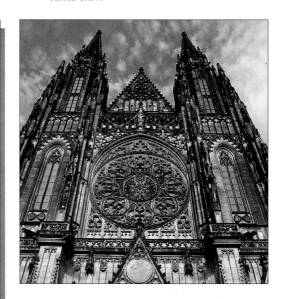

and off until World War II. Charles' later court architect **Peter Parler** took over from the first architect and managed to complete the eastern façade, but substantial work did not begin again until the 19th century. The oldest part of the exterior – the original Gothic of Parler – is therefore to the east, while the western façade and spires are the more recent Neo-Gothic.

The sheer scale of the interior is breathtaking, and much of the decoration and ornamentation is unashamedly exuberant. Peter Parler and Charles IV, together with a host of church dignitaries and civic luminaries, are depicted in the remarkably realistic Gothic sculptures that line the triforium in the inner choir.

Three chapels down from the main entrance to the cathedral is a stained-glass window depicting Sts Cyril and Methodius, in a characteristically distinctive design of 1931 by **Alfons Mucha**.

All the 22 side chapels contain much to admire, but the **Tomb of St John Nepomuk** in the ambulatory will be enjoyed by all lovers of excess. This emphatically Baroque edifice is made from vast quantities of silver and is the fruit of the Jesuits' campaign to have John made a saint. The man's corpse was exhumed and placed here after his canonization in 1729. Note the airborne angels who hold aloft the canopy over the tomb. The object on a platter is supposed to be St John's tongue, a reference to the saint's discretion: the legend is that he was killed because he refused to reveal to Václav IV what he had been told in confession by the queen.

The **Golden Gate** along from the tomb was for many centuries the main entrance to the cathedral – its exterior surface is decorated with a 14th-century mosaic of the Last Judgement, while inside it is carved with intertwined branches.

Parler's **Chapel of St Wenceslas** (*sv. Václav*) is a dazzling spectacle of semiprecious stones and vivid frescoes. A door within the chapel gives access to a higher chamber containing the Bohemian crown jewels: the seven keys to the door's seven locks are in seven different hands, and the jewels are not normally accessible to the public.

In the choir opposite the Wenceslas chapel is the **Habsburg Mausoleum** and the royal crypt, where lie the remains of some of the kings and queens of Bohemia.

> ### St Vitus
>
> This saint crops up everywhere in Prague, but little is known about him other than that he is venerated as a martyr. His legend – entirely lacking in evidence – asserts that he was put to death during the persecution of Diocletian. He was invoked against a number of illnesses, especially for epilepsy and chorea – which became known as **St Vitus' dance**. He was very popular in Germany, from whence his legend spread to Bohemia. His emblems are the cock and the dog, both of which can be seen in his statue on Charles Bridge.

Opposite: *Awesome St Vitus' Cathedral.*
Below: *St Vitus' Cathedral's ornate pulpit.*

Royal Palace **

Situated in the third courtyard on the south side of the cathedral, the **Royal Palace** (*Královský palác*) was home to the monarchs of Bohemia for 600 years until the 16th century, when it became an administrative headquarters and site of the Bohemian parliament. Its architectural archaeology begins in the cellars, which comprise the remnants of the original Romanesque palace of 1135. The Přemyslids and Charles IV built on top of this structure and the whole lot was finished off with the 15th-century **Vladislav Hall** (*Vladislavský sál*), an enormous and unforgettable Gothic

chamber. The first Bohemian kings were elected in this room and presidents of the republic since Masaryk's time have been sworn in beneath its graceful rib vaulting, including most recently Václav Havel in 1989. In medieval times it was also the scene of tournaments and jousts: the vaulted **Rider's Staircase** – with its wide, shallow steps and plenty of headroom – was designed to enable knights on horseback to pass in and out with ease.

After the hall, the best of the palace's many chambers include the **Bohemian Chancellery** (*Ceská kancelář*) and the medieval **parliament** (*Stará sněmovna*), the former being the scene of Prague's **Second Defenestration**. You can peer out of the window and imagine where the dung heap might have been that apparently saved the lives of the hapless Catholic envoys. The various chambers are decorated with large seals and coats of arms on ceilings and walls. The parliament was destroyed by the fire of 1541 and rebuilt 20 years later with rib vaulting echoing that of the Vladislav Hall. The oldest vaulting in the entire palace, however, was in the adjoining **All Saints' Chapel** (*kaple všech Svatých*), built by **Peter Parler** for Charles IV. The chapel was also damaged by the 1541 fire and much of it was rebuilt in the Baroque style.

BASILICA AND CONVENT OF ST GEORGE **

To the left of the Royal Palace and facing the cathedral is the Basilica of St George (*sv. Jiří*). Despite its red Baroque façade, the fabric of the basilica is scrupulously restored Romanesque, predating the cathedral. Founded in 921 by Prince Vratislav, the basilica and adjoining convent were rebuilt in 1142 after a fire.

The typically stark Romanesque interior has excellent acoustics and there are occasional concerts held here, with the Baroque chancel staircase used as a stage for the musicians. The most notable features inside the basilica are the **tombs of St Ludmilla and Vratislav** – the latter a simple wooden casket.

The **Convent of St George** (*Klášter sv. Jiří*) was the first such institution in Bohemia. Its first abbess was Mlada, great-granddaughter of Ludmilla and sister to Prince Boleslav II. In 1782 the convent was abolished and the building turned into barracks and storerooms, but in 1974 it was taken over by the National Gallery.

Above: *The Baroque exterior of the Basilica of St George.*

Old Bohemian Art Collection **

The collection – arranged in chronological order and in a fixed route for the viewer to follow through the building – covers the period between the 14th and 17th centuries, starting off in the crypt of the convent with **14th-century Czech art**. Most of these works are typical of the period: deeply symbolic and devotional panel paintings originally intended for the altars of churches. The Gothic convention of a gold background in which to set the colours and forms of the figures – the Virgin and Child, scenes from the life of Christ, or the portrait of a saint – somehow communicates the deep reverence which the painters (most unknown by name) must have felt for their subjects. Moving to the later Gothic on the ground floor, one can trace the development of such art from its initial abstractions and naiveties to an increased realism, where portraits – still suffused with the sacred – are painted with greater accuracy and attention to detail. The first floor also has many superb examples of Gothic woodcarving and sculpture, some of which is from the workshop of court architect **Peter Parler**.

The remainder of the collection is devoted to **Mannerist** art from the reign of Rudolf II and **Czech Baroque** art. **Ferdinand Brokof** is represented by some massive sculptures of Moorish warriors, as is his contemporary and rival **Matthias Braun**. **Jan Kupecký** – whose work is dotted all over Prague – is a Czech artist whose vibrant painting is also on show.

MANNERISM

The clash of **Reformation** and **Counter-Reformation** had unsettling artistic – as well as political – effects all over Europe. In painting and architecture, especially in Italy, it led to an abandonment by some artists of the Renaissance ideals of serenity, balance and classicism. Painting concentrated on the human figure, but often in strained, distorted poses and in compositions which were not immediately clear. Colours were more vivid – even harsh – in an attempt to convey heightened emotion. The turmoil and violence of religious and political conflict, so often experienced in Prague, have their counterparts in the Old Bohemian Collection.

EDWARD KELLEY

Edward Kelley and castle towers go together. It is said that the English **alchemist** poisoned himself in Prague Castle's White Tower after failing to find the secret of turning base metals into gold. He was also imprisoned in the great round tower of the castle of **Křivoklát** (see p. 108) for 2½ years for his alchemical failures. In attempting to escape from an upstairs window he broke his leg and had to have it amputated – the unfortunate man already lacked his ears, which had been cut off in England as a punishment for forgery.

Golden Lane and Castle Towers **

Behind the convent and beneath the castle wall, Golden Lane (*Zlatá ulička*) and its picturesque row of little houses – now souvenir shops – are mostly given over to the tourist trade. The houses were built in the 1500s for the castle guards and were later occupied by goldsmiths, from whom it is likely that the street gets its name.

The grim 15th-century **Dalibor Tower** (*Daliborka*) served as a prison and is named after its most famous inmate, **Dalibor of Kozojedy**. Locked up – so it is said – for sheltering outlawed serfs, Dalibor learned the violin while awaiting execution, his music attracting sympathy and gifts of food from people outside. The story later inspired Smetana's opera *Dalibor*.

The **Powder Tower** (*Prašná věž*) on Vikářská – north of the cathedral – became the laboratory for Rudolf II's alchemists after it ceased to be a bell foundry: in 1549 Prague's largest bell was made here for the cathedral. It contains a small exhibition relating to alchemy and astronomy.

CASTLE GARDENS **

Going back into the second courtyard of the castle, a small diversion beneath the stable block leads through the north gate and over the **Powder Bridge** (*Prašný most*) to the **Royal Garden** (*Královská zahrada*) and the **Belvedere** (*Belvedér*), or **Queen Anne's Summer Palace** (*Letohrádek královny Anny*) as it is also known. The gardens were first established in the 1530s by Ferdinand I and have since undergone many changes. The first tulips brought from Turkey were planted here, while

Below: *Picturesque Golden Lane.*

Rudolf II's zoo is now a restaurant. Today, the garden's fountains, lawns and its flower-beds are immaculately maintained and you can enjoy superb views over Prague and up toward the cathedral.

The Belvedere **

The Belvedere is one of the best examples of Renaissance architecture in northern Europe. Built for Anne, wife of Ferdinand I, and designed by the Genoese **Paolo della Stella**, construction began in 1538, was interrupted by the great fire of 1541 and was finally completed in 1564. It is a wonderfully harmonious building with a graceful Ionic colonnade – note how the windows and niches keep pace with the noble span of the arches and how the copper-clad roof is shaped like an inverted ship's hull. This lovely palace now hosts art exhibitions. The **Singing Fountain** (*Zpívající fontána*) in the Belvedere's small formal gardens emits a merry tinkle if you listen carefully.

Above: *The beautiful Royal Garden.*
Below: *The Royal Garden's musical Singing Fountain.*

South Gardens *

On the south side of the castle, Josip Plečnik's spiral **Bull Staircase** leads down from the third courtyard by the side of the Royal Palace to the South Gardens (*Jižní zahrady*), from which there are more spectacular views of the city. Plečnik's two observation pavilions and enormous granite basin in the **Paradise Garden** (*Rajská zahrada*) sit rather uneasily with the earlier Baroque pavilion and statuary elsewhere in the gardens.

Right: *Castle Square is lined with impressive palaces and mansions. This is the Archbishop's Palace, which dates from the middle of the 18th century.* **Opposite:** *Part of the sgraffito decoration of the Martinitz Palace.*

CASTLE SQUARE ***

Castle Square (*Hradčanské náměstí*) is just outside the main gates to the castle. Its grand palaces were built for the Catholic nobility in the early 17th century and are the result of reconstruction after the great fire of 1541 swept through the area.

To the left of the castle gates as you face the palace is the **Archbishop's Palace** (*Arcibiskupský palác*), whose extravagant Rococo façade dates from the 1760s but incorporates a portal from an earlier period. The palace has been the seat of the Catholic archbishops of Prague since 1621. Opposite, is the early-19th-century façade of the **Salm Palace** (*Salmovský palác*). Panoramic views can be had from the area between the Salm Palace and the castle entrance.

Schwarzenberg Palace **

The Schwarzenberg Palace (*Schwarzenberský palác*) next door is a superbly sgraffitoed building from 1563. The black and white design of the glorious façade deceives the eye into perceiving carved stone blocks, an effect which has made it one of Prague's most famous exteriors. The palace is now the **Military History Museum** (*Vojenské muzeum*), with a display of armaments and uniforms covering the centuries up to World War I.

MILITARY HISTORY MUSEUM

The Czechs have a long military history. Bohemia was plagued by war for centuries and the Czechs were obliged to be inventive in their technology – today's ubiquitous Semtex high explosive is the latest in a long line of successful exports. The museum has a fascinating collection of **armour** and **uniforms**, some of which are very dashing and seem more suited to socializing than warfare. You can also see the world's largest mortar, but if sophisticated instruments of death do not excite you there is always the splendid interior decoration of the palace itself, much of which is original.

On the western side of the square, the Czech Republic's foreign ministry is housed in the Baroque **Toscana Palace** (*Toskánský palác*), a monumental building completed in 1691. Its haughty appearance is softened by the delightful **Martinitz Palace** (*Martinický palác*) to its right, its early 17th-century exterior sporting a sgraffito picture depicting the Bible story of Joseph and his escape from Potiphar's wife.

Sternberg Palace ***

A passage next to the Archbishop's Palace leads to Prague's **National Gallery European Art Collection** in the Sternberg Palace (*Sternberský palác*). The palace itself is 18th century and built around a central courtyard, while the art collection arranged on its three floors spans painting and sculpture from their beginnings to the 20th century.

The ground floor contains **French art** of the **19th and 20th centuries** and is by far the most popular part of this valuable collection. At the time of writing there were plans to move part of the collection to the new National Gallery complex at Vleletržni palác, Dukelských hrdinů 47, Prague 7, but for convenience they are described here.

The first floor rooms commence with **Italian art** from 1300 to 1500 and comprise glorious Gothic panel paintings on sacred themes such as the Annunciation and the birth of Christ. There is also a fine selection of astonishingly beautiful **Eastern European and Byzantine icons**, plus a whole series of canvases by the Flemish artist **Breughel the Younger** and a large, rollicking *Haymaking* by **Breughel the Elder**.

The second floor begins with **German, Flemish** and **Dutch art** from around 1350 to 1700. The work of the German artist **Albrecht Dürer** was a personal favourite of Emperor Rudolf II, upon whose extensive art collection the National Gallery's catalogue

STERNBERG GALLERY HIGHLIGHTS

Other noteworthy paintings in the National Gallery's European Art Collection include:

• *Portrait of a Young Woman* from the 2nd century AD, artist unknown: earliest painting in collection.

• *The Old Fool* by **Lucas Cranach** (1472–1553): aged lust, youthful deception.

• *Dance at the Seaside* by **Edvard Munch** (1863–1944): Munch greatly influenced Czech art.

• *Head of Christ* by **El Greco** (1541–1614): haunting portrait.

• *Portrait of Eleanor of Toledo* by **Angelo Bronzino** (1503–72): intense Mannerist portrait.

• *St Jerome* by **Jacopo Tintoretto** (1518–94): sad, almost tearful portrait.

• *The Annunciation* by **Rembrandt** (1606–69): note the falling book.

is based. **Dürer's** *Feast of the Rosary* (1506) was the world's first non-Italian group painting. There are also superb canvases by **Lucas Cranach** – including remnants of the panel painting which once stood in St Vitus' Cathedral. Among the best examples of Dutch art in the collection are the works of **Rubens** – originally painted by the artist for the monks of the Church of St Thomas in the Lesser Quarter – and a typically profound study of contemplation by Rembrandt entitled *Scholar in his Study* (1634).

The second floor ends in a complete contrast with the resolutely modernist works of artists like **Ernst**, **Klimt** (an ambiguous and erotic canvas entitled *Virgin*), **Kokoschka** (including a view of Charles Bridge), **Munch** and **Schiele**.

THE LORETO LEGEND

The Loreto chapel owes its existence to the **Shrine of Loreto** in Italy, which became an important place of pilgrimage from the end of the 13th century. The legend grew up that the house of the Virgin Mary – scene of the Annunciation of the birth of Christ – was transported by angels from Nazareth to Loreto in 1278 after it was threatened by 'infidels'. The legend took hold of the Christian world and **copies** of the shrine were made all over Europe. The Counter-Reformation in Bohemia promoted the legend and 50 copies were made there and in Moravia.

Opposite top:
The Loreto Chapel.
Opposite bottom:
*Loretanska Street connects
Castle Square with
Loreto Square.*
Left: *Decoration along
Loreto Chapel's roofline.*

LORETO SQUARE
Loreto Chapel ★

Loretánská heads from the southwest corner of Castle Square to Loreto Square (*Loretánská náměstí*), site of the Loreto Chapel. This complex of buildings has been one of Bohemia's most significant places of pilgrimage since 1626, principally because of the Santa Casa, a copy of the house believed to be that of the Virgin Mary.

The Baroque façade of the Loreto dates from the 1720s and was added by the **Dientzenhofers** at the request of Ferdinand II. The large bell tower of the frontage contains 27 bells, which can be heard regularly throughout the day. The magnificent main portal incorporates statues of St Joseph and St John the Baptist and leads to the 17th-century cloisters, which were built to shelter the pilgrims who visited the shrine.

Projecting into the cloister courtyard is the Santa Casa itself, covered in stucco sculptures of biblical scenes and personages, and reliefs showing the life of the Virgin Mary. On the other side of the cloister wall stands the **Church of the Nativity** (*Kostel narození Páně*), also built by the Dientzenhofers. Not for the fainthearted, it contains many relics of saints, including the clothed skeletons of two of them, and paintings of martyrs such as St Agatha (carrying her severed breasts on a plate) and St Wilgefortis. The Loreto is open Tuesday–Sunday, 09:00–16:30, closing between 12:15 and 13:00.

ST WILGEFORTIS

The story of the fictional and rather bizarre figure of St Wilgefortis is that her father – the king of Portugal – wished her to marry the king of Sicily, even though she had vowed to remain a virgin. Her prayers for help were answered when she grew a beard: the king of Sicily understandably went off the marriage, but her father was so enraged that he had his daughter crucified. In England, Wilgefortis was invoked by women whose husbands were giving them trouble.

Above: *The twin spires of Strahov Monastery look out across the city from Petřín Hill.*

Cernín Palace *

On the other side of the square from the Loreto, and dominating everything around it, is the Cernín Palace (*Cernínský palác*), the largest palace in Prague. Some 150m (500ft) long, with diamond-cut stonework and a row of 30 enormous composite half-columns along its upper storeys, it looks more muscular than elegant. Its chequered career began in 1668, when it was built at enormous expense as the residence of the Ambassador of Venice. Since 1918 it has housed the country's Foreign Ministry and in 1948 was the scene of the mysterious death of Jan Masaryk.

STRAHOV MONASTERY **

Now once more a working monastery and museum, Strahov (*Strahovský klášter*) was founded in 1140. It functioned throughout the closure of monasteries in 1783, by claiming exemption as an educational establishment – a fair claim, since it had amassed Bohemia's greatest library of books. That same library is now 800 years old – kept in the monastery's Theological and Philosophical Halls, it is the principal reason for visiting Strahov.

The **Philosophical Hall** (*Filosofický sál*) was built in 1782 to house an influx of books from a dissolved monastery in Moravia. It is a splendidly welcoming room, full of the walnut patina of its enormous galleried Baroque bookcases and the leather bindings of the books themselves. The lovely fresco on the barrel-vaulted ceiling is by **Franz Maulbertsch** and is entitled *The Struggle of Mankind to Know Real Wisdom*. The **Theological Hall** (*Teologický sál*) is more intimate and possesses stucco-framed frescoes executed by one of the monks, plus some interesting 17th-century astronomical globes. Both rooms have an almost audible silence and are quite enchanting.

Also worth visiting is the monastery church – a highly decorated Baroque affair, its outer façade designed by **Anselmo Lurago** (son-in-law to Kilian Ignaz Dientzenhofer) in the 1750s. The interior is beautifully light and airy, with an unusual ceiling painted with scenes from the life of St Norbert, founder of the Premonstratensian Order.

Strahov's **Museum of Czech Literature** (*Památník národního písemnictví*) and its **Gallery** (*Strahovská obrazárna*) are both excellent, but probably only of interest to aficionados. The monastery garden can be explored for great views over the city and it connects with the adjoining expanse of Petřín Hill (*see* p. 56). Open Tuesday–Sunday, 09:00–12:00 and 12:30–17:00.

CREATURES OF THE DEEP

The antechamber to the Theological Hall and the Philosophical Hall is crammed with display cases containing all sorts of bizarre exhibits. There are various tentacled sea creatures and curiously shaped seashells, sitting cheek by jowl with old manuscripts and an odd assortment of bric à brac. It all seems rather out of keeping with the order and harmony of the libraries, but on busy days the display holds your attention while you wait for a glimpse of the main rooms.

Left: *The gorgeous interior of the Philosophical Hall.*

5
Josefov

Josefov – the Jewish Quarter of Prague – contains some beautiful and haunting traces of the historic community which lived and worked here. For centuries, the Jews of Prague had to endure the prejudice and oppression of their Christian neighbours. Enclosed in their own ghetto and subject to restrictive laws, it was not until 1784 and the reforms of Joseph II (after whom the Jewish Quarter was named) that some degree of freedom was attained. What remains of Josefov today survived the slum clearance project of the city authorities in the 1890s, when most of the area – which lacked all sanitation – was razed and replaced by Art Nouveau mansions for the wealthy.

Like Jews throughout Europe, the Prague Jews suffered appallingly under the Nazis. During the German occupation of Prague, Jewish people were transported to the purpose-built ghetto of Terezín and thence to extermination camps: some 36,000 were to die there. The historic synagogues and cemetery of Josefov survive today only because of Hitler's ghoulish plan to preserve Prague's old ghetto as a museum of an extinct race. There is still a small Jewish community in Prague and some synagogues remain places of worship.

Pařížská ulice heads north from Old Town Square practically dividing Josefov in half. Its shops and restaurants inhabit buildings erected in the 1890s with many fine examples of Art Nouveau architecture along its length.

DON'T MISS

*** Old-New Synagogue: oldest functioning synagogue in Europe; Rabbi Löw's chair.
** Decorative Arts Museum: collection of Bohemian arts and crafts: glass; jewellery; furniture.
** Old Jewish Cemetery: fascinating historic burial place.
** Pařížská ulice: splendid Art Nouveau buildings.
** Pinkas Synagogue: memorial to the Czech-Jewish victims of the Holocaust.
* Jewish Town Hall: with Hebrew clock and tower.

Opposite: *A detail of the Town Hall in Prague's Jewish Quarter.*

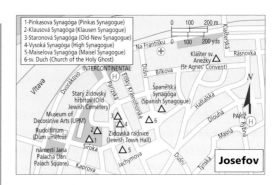

1-Pinkasova Synagóga (Pinkas Synagogue)
2-Klausová Synagóga (Klausen Synagogue)
3-Staronová Synagóga (Old-New Synagogue)
4-Vysoká Synagóga (High Synagogue)
5-Maiselova Synagóga (Maisel Synagogue)
6-sv. Duch (Church of the Holy Ghost)

THE GOLEM

A leading scholar of the Talmud in the 16th century, **Rabbi Löw's** prestige was such that he was believed to possess miraculous powers. It was said that he created the artificial man called the golem by moulding him in clay from the Vltava. The golem was brought to life each time the rabbi placed in its mouth a small stone with a magical Hebrew inscription. The tales are embroidered on each time they are told, but they always end with the golem running amok and the rabbi hiding the lifeless body in the roof of the Old-New Synagogue – where it remains to this day.

Below: *The distinctive gable of the historic Old-New Synagogue.*

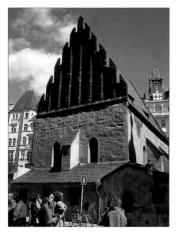

THE JEWISH QUARTER
Old-New Synagogue ***

This synagogue (*Staronová synagóga*) on Pařížská is the oldest functioning synagogue in Europe – building commenced in the 1270s – and the most important Jewish centre in Prague. Easily recognized by its 14th-century stepped-brick gable, it was originally called simply the New Synagogue, but became known as the Old-New after another synagogue was built nearby (it was later destroyed).

You can go inside the synagogue by buying a ticket from the ticket office opposite the synagogue entrance. The main hall of the interior is bounded in part by **women's galleries**, which were added in the 18th century to allow them a view of proceedings. The doorway to the hall has a beautiful **tympanum** of carved grape clusters and vine leaves: the 12 bunches of grapes represent the 12 tribes of Israel. The rib-vaulted **main hall** contains the **Ark** – a sort of shrine which holds the sacred scrolls of the Torah (the first five books of the Jewish Bible). This is the holiest place in the synagogue, surrounded by candles and topped with a lovely 13th-century tympanum carved with leaves. Next to it is the **chair of the Chief Rabbi**, indicated by a small Star of David on the wall above. **Rabbi Löw** – creator of the mythical golem – used to sit here.

Town Hall *

The Josefov **Town Hall** (*Židovská radnice*) across from the synagogue had a Baroque facelift in 1763, but its core structure is from the 1570s. Note the Hebrew clock on the gable: because Hebrew is read from right to left, its hands rotate 'anti-clockwise'. The adjoining **High Synagogue** (*Vysoká synagóga*) on Červená was once part of the Town Hall complex, but they were separated in the 19th century. The synagogue is not open to the public.

Above: *The most relaxing way to see the sights.*

Other Synagogues

South of the Town Hall on Maiselova is the **Maisel Synagogue** (*Maiselova synagóga*). The original building was constructed at the end of the 16th century for Jewish mayor **Mordechai Maisel**, but was destroyed by a great fire which swept through Josefov in 1689. This new structure replaced the original, although the Neo-Gothic crenelations are early 20th century. It contains a fascinating exhibition relating to Prague Jewry and also protects the oldest tombstone from the Jewish cemetery: dating from 1439, it belonged to the poet **Avigdor Caro**.

Worth a look for its distinctive Moorish exterior alone, the 19th-century **Spanish Synagogue** (*Španělská synagóga*) on Vězeňská also has a wonderfully ornate interior. The **Pinkas Synagogue** (*Pinkasova synagóga*) stands beside the Old Jewish Cemetery with its entrance on Široká. Built in 1479 and rebuilt many times, its memorial interior is now inscribed with the names of all those Czech Jews who died in the Holocaust. There is also an ancient well and ritual bath discovered during renovation work.

> ### THE MIGHTY MAYOR
>
> **Mordechai Maisel** was Emperor Rudolf II's minister of finance and mayor of the Jewish Quarter. He was one of the richest men in Bohemia, amassing most of his wealth by lending money to the emperor to finance his expensive campaigns against the Turks. Maisel's money was used to build the **Maisel Synagogue**, originally as a private place of prayer for the Maisel family, but it also financed several public synagogues (including the Klausen), the **Town Hall** and other civic works. A Josefov hero, he is buried in the Old Jewish Cemetery near Rabbi Löw, his contemporary.

Above: *Crowded grave-stones struggle for space in the Old Jewish Cemetery.*

Old Jewish Cemetery ✶✶
You're unlikely to come across a more crowded cemetery than this one in Josefov. For 600 years until the late 18th century the Jewish population of Prague was buried here. Thousands of ornately carved snaggle-toothed tombstones cover the uneven ground, where bodies can lie as many as 12 deep in places – the tomb inscriptions provide valuable source material for historians. First thing in the morning (the quietest period) there is no more moving testimony to the scale and vibrancy of the Jewish culture that once blossomed in Prague.

The most famous person buried here is **Rabbi Löw**. His tomb is almost opposite the entrance to the cemetery, along the west wall and marked by a plaque. Visitors place pebbles and written wishes on his grave as a mark of respect. Other noteworthy tombs include that of **Rabbi David Oppenheim**, a few metres away from Rabbi Löw's, who collected thousands of old Hebrew manuscripts and prints before he died in 1736. His collection is now in the Bodleian Library in Oxford, UK. The medieval-looking **ceremonial hall** (*Obřadní síň*) was built by the Jewish Burial Society and contains a deeply moving exhibition of pictures drawn in the Jewish ghetto at Terezín. Adjoining the hall is the Baroque **Klausen Synagogue**, which has a fine barrel-vaulted interior and rich stucco work. It was built in the 1690s on the site of some Jewish schools and houses of prayer (known as *klausen*) which were destroyed in a fire of 1689. The synagogue exhibits old Jewish prints and manuscripts.

> **CARVED IN STONE**
>
> The tombstones in the **Old Jewish Cemetery** feature several motifs and devices, and particular symbols dating from the late 16th century indicate the family name, profession or cultural status of the deceased. Some of the most common are scissors for a tailor and a knife for a butcher. A bear stands for a member of the Brown family, a pair of hands for the Cohens and a fish for the Fishers. Women are often symbolized in more detail: a lone woman signifies a virgin, but if she has her left hand raised it means she was a virgin bride.

Decorative Arts Museum (UPM) ✶✶
Next to the western perimeter of the cemetery, in a 19th-century Neo-Renaissance building designed by **Josef**

Schulz, the UPM contains a vast and varied collection which includes particularly fine examples of Art Nouveau and Avant Garde artistry dating from the 1890s to the 1930s, plus splendid Bohemian glasswork and extensive displays of furniture. There are always interesting and lively temporary exhibitions, making the museum one of the most fascinating and provocative in Prague. The building has a superb interior with richly decorated stairwells and ceilings.

St Agnes' Convent **

Tucked away to the northwest and technically outside Josefov, the twin convents of St Agnes have been heavily restored since they fell into disrepair in 1782, but they remain important examples of early Gothic architecture. The cloister vaulting dates from the 14th century, and there are associated churches and chapels to explore, but the chief attraction is the **art gallery** in the rooms off the cloister and on the first floor. Devoted to Czech art of the 19th century, it includes evocative Prague cityscapes, subtle portraits and portrayals of incidents from Czech history and myth.

RUDOLFINUM

On Jan Palach Square (*Náměstí Jana Palacha*) in the west of Josefov, the Rudolfinum is the home of the Czech Philharmonic and boasts an excellent grand café. One of the great buildings of the 19th-century **Czech National Revival**, it was built in 1884 to a design by **Josef Zítek** and **Josef Schulz**. Originally an arts centre, it was afterwards used as the Czech parliament before the Nazis closed it. The curving exterior balustrade is decorated with statues of composers and artists – including the Jewish Mendelssohn. The Nazis took exception to the statue, but accidentally removed that of Wagner (Hitler's favourite composer) by mistake.

Left: *The peaceful cloisters of St Agnes' Convent lead to a fine collection of paintings and sculpture.*

6
Nové Město

Founded in 1348 by Charles IV, **New Town** (*Nové Město*) is the commercial and business centre of Prague and its most lively part: shops, cafés, bars and restaurants all compete for space along New Town's elegant boulevards and squares. Major redevelopment in the 19th century made New Town the most architecturally varied area of Prague, with, it seems, superb examples of Art Nouveau and modernist styles on every corner. New Town is also the part of Prague where so much of the city's recent history was made: key events in the Prague Spring and the Velvet Revolution took place here.

WENCESLAS SQUARE *

Prague's most famous square is the hub of New Town, and is in fact less a square than a long, tree-lined boulevard. Wenceslas Square (*Václavské náměstí*) points southeast from Old Town, a bustling, vibrant place of large hotels, discos, clubs and stores. In medieval times it was a horse market, but there is no sign of that now – the square's oldest building is from the 18th century, while the rest were constructed predominantly over the last 100 years.

In November 1989, as successive communist regimes fell in Eastern Europe, Wenceslas Square hit the world headlines as the venue of nightly mass protests against the government: a quarter of a million people crammed into the area. On 27 November Prague was paralysed in a national general strike called by Civic Forum, the opposition coalition led by Václav Havel. The next day, the communist government collapsed.

DON'T MISS

*** Charles Square: park and historic buildings.
** Church of St John Nepomuk on the Rock: unusual Dientzenhofer masterpiece; mirrored chapel.
** National Theatre: magnificent auditorium for concerts.
** Municipal House: Prague's greatest Art Nouveau building.
* Dvořák Museum: delightful Dientzenhofer villa and garden.
* Wenceslas Square: historic heart of the Velvet Revolution.

Opposite: *The proud Wenceslas Monument.*

Opposite: *The entrance to the Hotel Evropa .*

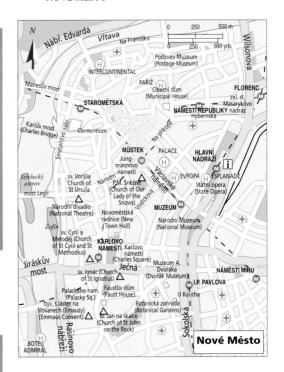

Nové Město

At the northern end of the square the most prominent building is the **Koruna Palace** (*palác Koruna*), which was built in 1914. The rich ornamentation of this shop and office complex ends in a crowned corner turret.

There are lots of sights around the square, but here are some of the more interesting to look out for. The **Peterkův dům** (no. 12) dates from the 1890s and was one of the first Art Nouveau buildings in Prague. It was designed by **Jan Kotěra**, while the **Hotel Juliš** (no. 22) was designed by **Pavel Janák**. Almost opposite the hotel – on the corner with Jindřišská – is the **Assicurazioni Generali** building. This modern study in Baroque (now the Polish Cultural Institute) was the insurance office in which **Franz Kafka** worked briefly in 1906–7. This attractive building might well wince at its neighbour, a dour 1970s department store.

Václavské náměstí (Wenceslas Square)

The five-storey **Wiehl House** is on the opposite corner with Vodičkova ulice. Built in 1896 by **Antonín Wiehl**, the façade is immediately recognizable from its Art Nouveau sgraffito depicting full-length figures, lush vegetation and *trompe-l'oeil* friezes. Next door is **Melantrich House**. It was on the first floor balcony of this building that Havel and Dubček appeared to the assembled crowds during the Velvet Revolution. Close to Melantrich House is the **Lucerna Palace**, one of Prague's vast shopping arcades. This one includes a concert hall and cinema and was designed in Moorish style in the early 1900s.

Immerse yourself in the charm of an earlier era by stopping for a drink at the slightly faded but still elegant **Hotel Evropa**, opposite the Lucerna. The lavishly ornate Art Nouveau exterior – replete with gilding and sgraffito – is matched by an equally exuberant interior, where the fittings – mirrors and panelling, bars and lights – are mostly original.

In the middle of the southern end of the square, in front of the National Museum, is the statue of St Wenceslas. A statue of the saint has stood in the square since the late 1600s, though the present **Wenceslas Monument** was placed here in 1912. Cast in bronze, the huge figure of Wenceslas astride his steed is surrounded

by the statues of various other Czech saints. If anyone feels like making an impromptu speech, this is the place to do it: the monument is one of the city's focal points for protest and oratory. An unofficial **Memorial to the Victims of Communism** (*Obětem komunismu*) sits in front of the monument: the wreaths, photographs and crosses are simple and eloquent.

Above: *The National Museum is lit up at night.*

ART NOUVEAU RAILWAY

Prague's **Wilsonova** railway station (*Hlavní nádraží*) lies to the north of the State Opera, on Wilsonova ulice. The modern subterranean part of the station gives no clue to the glories above. Completed in 1901, the original building is a vast structure in the great tradition of the European railways and the age of steam. A massive glass dome caps an interior with splendid Art Nouveau design features – which include garlanded pilasters and allegorical sculptural work – in creams, blues and browns. Even the balustrading – made from brass and wrought iron – is in a sweeping design suggestive of streamlined speed.

National Museum **

The vast Neo-Renaissance **National Museum** (*Národní muzeum*), complete with glass dome, dominates the southern end of the square. Designed by **Josef Schulz** in 1890 in conscious emulation of the great museums of Paris and Vienna, the building is also one of Prague's best testimonies to the Czech revival in the arts. The imposing entrance is lined with allegorical figures, culminating in the personifications of History and Natural History, two of the subjects to which the museum is principally dedicated. Inside, the wonderful **main staircase** has clusters of brass lamps along its balustrading and is framed by elegantly decorated porticoes of marble Corinthian half-columns. At its top – beneath the glass dome – is the museum's **Pantheon**: statues and busts of Czech scholars and artists. The building itself is in fact the museum's chief highlight: although the standard of temporary exhibitions has improved somewhat since 1989, the permanent exhibits are rather lacklustre.

State Opera *

The terrible scar of Wilsonova (a five-lane highway) means that the **State Opera** (*Státní opera*) – east of the museum – now stands in noble isolation next to the brutalist former Federal Assembly. Built in 1888, it was called the New German Theatre and was intended to rival the Czech National Theatre which had just been built on the banks of the Vltava. Its wonderful façade – Neoclassical in design – has six Corinthian columns supporting a pediment filled with a swirling frieze depicting Dionysus, the Greek god of wine, and Thalia, the classical muse of comedy. Inside, the magnificent auditorium is all gilt stucco and red plush, with many of the original paintings from the theatre's opening still in place – a night at the opera here would make for a memorable evening.

EAST OF WENCESLAS SQUARE

From the northeast end of Wenceslas Square Na příkopě ('On the moat') marks the official boundary between Old and New Town. There are some fine Art Nouveau buildings to admire, on the street itself and in **Republic Square** (*Náměstí Republiky*), the square to which it is joined.

Above: *Simple but moving, a Memorial to the Victims of Communism.*
Below: *The National Museum's impressive staircase and Pantheon.*

Municipal House **

Linked to the Powder Gate (*see* p. 37) by an arch, the splendid **Municipal House** (*Obecní dům*) stands on the site of King Vladislav Jagiello's 15th-century royal court and is undoubtedly Prague's best Art Nouveau building.

Completed in 1911 as an arts and cultural centre, the building was designed by **Osvald Polívka** and **Antonín Balšánek**. The domed façade has a large semi-circular mosaic entitled *Tribute to Prague* and is richly decorated with stucco and statuary. But it is the inside of the building that is particularly worth seeing, for virtually every fitment in every room is original: if you dine in one of

ALFONS MUCHA

Alfons Mucha (1860–1939) won international recognition with his **Art Nouveau posters** and went on to design stamps and banknotes for the state of Czechoslovakia. He is regarded by some as no more than a kitschy popularizer of Art Nouveau, yet his work adorns outstanding buildings such as **St Vitus' Cathedral** and the **Municipal House** – his cathedral window has been described as static and lifeless, but his Municipal House frescoes depicting civic virtues are dynamic and arresting. 'Serious artist' or workaday graphicist, Mucha's style is instantly recognizable and Prague would have been less interesting without him.

the cafés and restaurants you'll be able to view everything in comfort. You may also be able to join a guided tour to view some of the outstanding sculptural detailing of **Alfons Mucha**, plus the paintings and mosaics of the greatest Czech artists of the day. The **Smetana Hall** is the most important part of the complex: the city's largest concert venue, it is the scene of the first concert in the annual Prague Spring Festival.

The Hibernians

The large Neoclassical building opposite the Municipal House is the Hibernians (*U hybernů*), which was built as a customs house at the beginning of the 19th century. Its unusual name refers to the order of Irish Franciscans whose church previously occupied the site. Walking down the similarly named Hybernská, you will come across the Art Nouveau Hotel Central, which was built in 1900 and designed by the architects responsible for the Hotel Evropa. Masarykovo nádraží – built in 1845 as the city's first railway station – is a little further on, while on the opposite side of the road from the station is the Café Arco, which was once one of Kafka's watering holes.

WEST OF WENCESLAS SQUARE

Off the northwest end of Wenceslas Square, **Jungmann Square** (*Jungmannovo náměstí*) is named after the famous writer and scholar **Josef Jungmann** (1773–1847), whose statue is in the middle of the square. There are some interesting buildings here, the most prominent of which is the **Adria Palace** on the south side. Built in 1925 for an insurance company, it is partly in the Rondo-Cubist style pioneered by its designers **Pavel Janák** and **Josef**

Below: *Part of the Municipal House complex, the impressive Smetana Hall is Prague's largest concert venue.*

Left: *Národní Street,*
a bustling thoroughfare
leading west from
Wenceslas Square, is
lined with some splendid
examples of Art Nouveau.

Zasche. Rondo-Cubism was a deliberate attempt at developing an architecture symbolic of the new Republic of Czechoslovakia, and as the name suggests made great use of curves and semi-circular geometric forms. **Civic Forum** was based in the Adria Palace during the Velvet Revolution.

If you look carefully, you may also find a 1912 Cubist streetlamp in the eastern corner of the square, beyond which is the unfinished colossus of the **Church of Our Lady of the Snows** (*Kostel Panny Marie Sněžné*), built in 1397. Intended to commemorate the coronation of Charles IV, only the presbytery of what was going to be a vast church was finished. Some 33m (110ft) in height, the structure suffered in the Hussite wars and was later neglected before its interior underwent a Baroque conversion.

The impressively extravagant altar and the sheer scale of the interior are worth admiring. Next door is a small public park, which was formerly the herb garden of a Franciscan monastery.

Národní heads west from the square. There are some fine Art Nouveau buildings along the street: watch out especially for number 7 (which spells *'Praha'* with its top windows) and number 9. Opposite them is the **Church of St Ursula** (*sv. Voršila*), an early Baroque church built in 1678.

TWO MUSEUMS

In the north of the New Town two museums well off the tourist route stand rather isolated and forlorn. The **Postage Museum** (*Poštovní muzeum*) on Nové Mlýny has a large collection of stamps from all over the world. There are some outstanding examples of Czech stamps, many of which were produced by leading artists such as Alfons Mucha. The **Prague Museum** (*Muzeum hlavní města Prahy*) on Na poříčí inhabits an 1890s Neo-Renaissance house and contains an eclectic display relating to the city, including a paper model of Prague made in 1834 by Antonín Langweil.

TRAM 22

This is *the* tram for seeing the sights and for enjoying the best ride on the system. Starting off in the eastern suburbs, tram 22 wends its way through Míru and Charles Squares before turning left on Národní and crossing the river to the Lesser Quarter. A short straight leads to Lesser Quarter Square, after which there are the chicanes of Letenská. The tram then ascends to the castle via a series of hairpin bends and climbs still further to Strahov. An enormously long and fast straight takes it past Břevnov Monastery to its terminus at White Mountain.

National Theatre **

The greatest landmark on Národní is at the western end of the street. The National Theatre (*Národní divadlo*) was probably *the* symbol of what it meant to be Czech in the 19th century. The theatre was paid for by public subscription, but days before its official opening in 1881 the theatre was totally destroyed by fire. Two years later a new building was completed under the supervision of **Josef Schulz** (who designed the National Museum) and the first performance given there was appropriately a Smetana opera. The theatre still presents mainly Czech plays, opera and ballets.

The northern portal and the entire roofline of the theatre are covered in allegorical statuary, while the exterior of the top-most roof is coloured a vibrant blue dotted with silver stars (symbolizing the creative heights which all artists should aim for). All the major Czech artists of the period contributed work on the sumptuous interior decoration, which includes massive ceiling frescoes depicting the arts and a gorgeous stage curtain of reds and golds. In 1983 a controversial extension to the theatre called the **New Stage** (*Nová scená*) was completed: love it or hate it, its series of gigantic glass boxes certainly catches the eye.

Below: *The National Theatre has a unique blue roof studded with stars.*

Left: *The monumental glass construction of the New Stage, completed in 1983, forms part of the National Theatre.*

SOUTH TOWARD VYSEHRAD

Vodičkova connects Wenceslas Square with Charles Square: number 22 – a university faculty building – is a superb example of red sgraffito.

   Charles Square (*Karlovo náměstí*) was designed as a cattle market in the 14th century, but today it has a graceful park at its centre – albeit surrounded by busy roads. There are fine buildings on the perimeter of the square.

New Town Hall *

To the northeast side of the square is Nové Město's **New Town Hall** (*Novoměstská radnice*), constructed in the 15th and 16th centuries and the site of Prague's **First Defenestration**. The Gothic design includes some tracery on the prominent gables of the building, while inside there is a splendid hall with strikingly painted ceiling beams. The hall is used for exhibitions and other events, so it should be possible to see inside.

Church of St Ignatius **

The **Church of St Ignatius** (*sv. Ignáce*) is one of Prague's most elaborately decorated Baroque churches built by the Jesuits during the Counter-Reformation. The curlicued exterior features statues of St Ignatius of Loyola – the founder of the Jesuits – while the church's interior is a riot of stucco and gilt ornamentation. The adjoining former **Jesuit College** (*Jezuitská kolej*) occupies half of the eastern

---

ELISKA KRASNOHORSKA

At the northern end of Charles Square is an unobtrusive statue of a woman, placed there in 1931. Eliška Krásnohorská was born Eliška Pechová in Prague in 1847. She became a poet and formed an association with Smetana, and would be described as the unsung heroine of their partnership if it were not for the fact that her words are sung regularly throughout the world. She wrote the librettos for many of his operas, including **The Kiss** (*Hubička*) and **The Secret** (*Tajemství*), and it is on these works that her fame chiefly rests. She died in Prague in 1926.

Above: *Taking time out to peruse the papers.*

side of Charles Square. It was finished in 1702, but only 70 years later the Jesuits left Prague, and their college has been used as a hospital ever since.

Off the western side of the square and along Resslova is the Baroque **Church of St Cyril and St Methodius** (*sv. Cyril a Metoděje*), built in the 1730s. Originally a Catholic church, it was closed in the 1780s. After restoration work in the 1930s it was given to the Czechoslovak Orthodox Church, when it was rededicated to Cyril and Methodius.

In June 1942 seven of the agents involved in the assassination of Nazi leader Reinhard Heydrich took refuge in the Church of St Cyril and St Methodius. Betrayed by a member of the Czech resistance, the agents put up a stout fight as hundreds of German troops attempted to shoot, bomb, smoke and even flood their way in to the crypt where the agents were based. After some six hours, the agents – by now desperately short of ammunition – committed suicide rather than allow themselves to be captured and interrogated.

The crypt of the church contains a moving exhibition and memorial for the events that took place there in June 1942. On the crypt's outer wall there is a memorial plaque near some bullet holes from German machine guns.

Church of St John Nepomuk on the Rock **

South of Charles Square on Vyšehradská, the **Church of St John Nepomuk on the Rock** (*sv. Jan Nepomuck´y na skalce*) is yet another **Dientzenhofer** Baroque masterpiece, this time by **Kilian Ignaz** alone. Smaller than many of the city's Baroque churches, it was finished in 1738, though the grand stairway leading up to the main entrance was not built until the 1770s. The bravura of the church's façade – so sinuous it's difficult

---

FAUST HOUSE

The association of Faust House (no. 40, Charles Square) with alchemy and the occult is what gives it its name and reputation. The houses on this site have witnessed the goings-on of **Prince Václav of Opava** – a 14th-century alchemist – and the infamous **Edward Kelley**. The present Baroque building is also the site of Prague's version of the Faust legend, which tells of a student who finds money belonging to the devil and has to forfeit his soul in return for wealth. Unperturbed by these stories, a surgery on the ground floor preserves the building's historic links with chemistry.

to believe stone is involved at all – is matched by the unusual interior, based on the octagon. The generous sweep of the frescoed half-domes rests on an intricately carved entablature, while the warm wood colours of the organ case contrast beautifully with the creams and whites of the stone pillars that enclose it. Notice, too, the wooden statue on the high altar, which is a replica of Brokof's famous statue of St John Nepomuk on Charles Bridge.

Slavonic Monastery *
For a complete change from Baroque architecture, have a look at the **Slavonic Monastery** (*Klášter na Slovanech*) opposite. Largely destroyed by American bombing in World War II, not much of the Gothic-looking structure is original, but the two concrete spires are an interesting and imaginative modern addition to the architectural heritage of Prague. Some medieval frescoes – mostly badly damaged – survived the attack.

Botanical Gardens *
South of the church at the end of Vyšehradská there are Prague's late 19th-century **Botanical Gardens** (*Botanická zahrada*), the vast glass-houses of which were constructed in 1938. In summer this is a charming place to wander, the terraced gardens providing some much-needed shade.

Below: *Střelecký ostrov island, a fine place for a stroll.*

ALONG THE RIVER

All roads heading west from Charles Square lead to the Vltava River, from where the islands of **Střelecký ostrov** and **Zofín** can be reached. Both are pleasant places to stroll, but Zofín (named after its concert hall) is the best. Its attractive gardens can be crowded with walkers in summer, but there are also rowing boats for hire and balls and concerts are held here throughout the year.

Rašínovo nábřeží – south along the river – is lined with rows of apartment houses and mansions dating from the turn of the 20th century. Many are magnificent and ornately decorated but none are open to the public.

Rašín Building

Also on this road is possibly the most famous building constructed in Prague during the 1990s: the Rašín building, known as **Fred and Ginger** because its flared glass-curtained tower looks like the swirling skirts of a female dancer as she clings to her partner. Designed by **Frank Gehry** and **Vlado Milunić** (Canadian and Czech, respectively) it is situated next to a turn-of-the-century apartment block designed by Václav Havel's grandfather: the President and his family lived in one of the apartments. Whatever one thinks of the postmodernist building – and both its appearance and prominent location have certainly earned it some controversy – it is heartening that Prague's traditional progressivism in architecture continues.

Below: *The Michna Summer Palace, home of the Dvořak Museum.*

Palacký Square

Palacký Square (*Palackého náměstí*) lies to the south of Fred and Ginger and is dedicated to the historian and politician **František Palacký**, one of the key figures in the Czech national revival of the 19th century. His Art Nouveau monument in the middle of the square – designed by Stanislav Sucharda – was finished in 1912. The monument depicts the world of imagination – symbolized by the figures at the top – and the massive form of Palacký himself.

Left: *The U Kalicha pub benefits from its associations with* The Good Soldier Svejk.

Dvořák Museum *

On Ke Karlovu to the east of Charles Square, the Dvořák Museum (*Muzeum Antonína Dvořáka*) is well worth visiting, regardless of any interest in the composer. The museum inhabits a lovely Baroque villa originally called the Michna Summer Palace, built in 1720 by the ubiquitous **Kilian Ignaz Dientzenhofer**. The building and its gardens were neglected in the 19th century, but happily have since been restored. All the garden statues and vases are from the workshops of **Matthias Braun**. The two-storey villa's charming façade is a delightful combination of ochre plasterwork and yellow stone, while the tiered roof is punctured by an exquisite bull's-eye window.

The museum displays scores and editions of the composer's works, but there is not much in the way of personal memorabilia, though you can enjoy recordings of Dvorak's music as you wander through the building.

U Kalicha Pub *

Around the corner from the museum on Na bojistí is the **U Kalicha pub**, immortalized in the opening pages of **Jaroslav Hašek's** novel *The Good Soldier Svejk* – it is here that the unwitting Svejk is arrested for the assassination of Archduke Ferdinand. The pub is very popular with tourists, so if you fancy a drink it pays to get there early.

JAROSLAV HASEK

The creator of *The Good Soldier Svejk* was born in Prague in 1883. A prolific novelist, he published the four-volume Svejk – set at the time of the slow disintegration of the Austro-Hungarian empire – in 1920–23, and the novel was translated into English in 1930. Non-Czech readers who may be unfamiliar with Czech history might miss the understated nationalism that permeates the novel, but will still see the humour of the story in which the humble soldier Svejk blithely continues on his way, sowing confusion and disarray in the path of authority. Hašek died in Lipnice in 1923.

7
Vyšehrad and the Suburbs

Prague city centre is so beautiful that the suburbs – attractive as many of them are – may seem a little ordinary in comparison. However, they do contain lots of interesting things to see which are easy to find – the trams and metro can whisk you to outlying areas in a few minutes, after which it is often no more than a short walk to your destination.

The suburbs are where you can see the everyday life of Prague. The streets are busy with shoppers commuting to and from the city centre, while the local food shops and outdoor markets also do a brisk trade. In the eastern suburbs you'll come across some attractive garden squares, many of them with the local church at their centre. The turn-of-the-century apartment blocks that line some once-elegant boulevards have usually seen better days, but gradually they are being restored to their former glory. The northern and western suburbs contain some lovely parks and open spaces, plus some superb villas.

These outlying areas of the city can also provide a pleasant change of pace. There are fewer crowds to contend with and there are quiet, secluded spots where you can rest and recuperate.

Vyšehrad

Vyšehrad (literally 'castle on the heights') is a rocky eminence next to the southern boundary of New Town. It overlooks the Vltava and has a superb view along the river to the cathedral, which is about 3km (2 miles) away. Legend has it that Vyšehrad was the first area of Prague to

Bubeneč		
Hradčany		Karlín
Malá Strana	Josefov	Žižkov
	Staré Město	
Smíchov	Nové Město	Vinohrady
Radlice	Vyšehrad	Nusle

DON'T MISS

*** Troja Summer Palace: superb Italian-style villa in formal French gardens.
** Stromovka Park: one of Prague's largest parks; woods, gardens, summer palace.
** Vyšehrad Cemetery: Art Nouveau headstones, statuary; famous graves.
** Vyšehrad Fortress: historic fortress remains in parkland, stunning views.
* National Technical Museum: superb museum of transport, industry and science.
* Zoo: ideal for youngsters.

Opposite: *The Italianate Troja Palace, near Stromovka.*

PRINCESS LIBUSE

Some time in the 9th century, the mythical figure of Princess Libuše was supposedly asked by her subjects to take a husband to rule over them. Libuše set off on horseback and married a man named **Přemysl**, with whom she founded the Přemyslid dynasty. She is also said to have stood on the rock of **Vyšehrad** and seen a vision of a great city on the banks of the Vltava. A voice told her to lay the first stone of the city on Hradčany, thus establishing the castle. Her story became the basis of Smetana's opera *Libuše*.

Above: *The Church of Sts Peter and Paul.*
Opposite: *One of the church's door panels.*

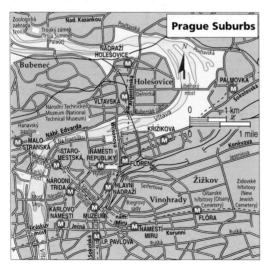

be settled. Archaeological evidence, however, suggests that settlement commenced no earlier than the medieval period, when Vratislav II built a fortress in the 11th century. Charles IV later insisted on commencing his coronation procession from the hill and built fortified walls connecting Vyšehrad with New Town. In 1420, the medieval fortress was destroyed in the Hussite wars. In the 19th century, nationalists made Vyšehrad *the* symbol of Czech solidarity and heritage: patriotic gatherings were regularly held here, and Smetana elaborated on the myth of Vyšehrad in his opera *Libuše*. Many of the places of interest in and around Vyšehrad date from this period.

Vyšehrad Fortress **

The fortress remains are set in a peaceful landscaped park at the summit of the hill. The walls and ramparts can be wandered around at leisure: the western entrance to the fortress is the 17th-century **Tábor Gate**, adjacent to which are the remains of Charles IV's 14th-century fortifications. Two further gates are the original Gothic **Spička Gate** and the 17th-century **Leopold Gate**.

The Romanesque **Rotunda of St Martin** (*sv. Martina*) – heavily restored in the 19th century – is the only remnant of the original medieval fortress. The western side of the fortress is rather more spectacular: the hill turns abruptly into a steep cliff above the Vltava, and the remains of the fortress cling to the side of the hill. There are great views here and you also have the chance to peer into **Libuše's Baths**. This seemingly impregnable position is what made the idea of building defences so attractive. Within the fortress area there is a small museum and a permanent exhibition in a Neo-Gothic deanery.

On the slopes to the northwest is the **Church of St Peter and St Paul** (*sv. Petr a Pavel*), built in the 1880s on the site of an 11th-century basilica: remains of the earlier structure are visible in the church. The twin spires of this Neo-Gothic edifice were added in the early 1900s and can be seen everywhere on Vyšehrad. The groups of statues on the lawn before the church are taken from Palacký Bridge, where they were damaged by US aerial bombardment in World War II.

Vyšehrad

Vyšehrad Cemetery **

The patriotic agitation of the 19th century led to the establishment of this small national cemetery in 1869, laid out to the north and east of the church. Within its high retaining walls the cemetery is excellently maintained and the Art Nouveau design of the graves and statuary makes the cemetery a delight to explore. Many of the country's greatest artists and scholars are buried here, at least those who were prominent in the nationalist cause – there is a plan of the famous graves at the entrance to the cemetery. The Prague Spring Music Festival commences every year with a procession from **Smetana's** graveside to the Municipal House in New Town. **Dvořák's** grave is a grand affair in the cemetery's memorial arcade, which was built in 1898. The monumental **Slavín Memorial** commemorates some 50 Czech artists, among them **Alfons Mucha** and the sculptor **Ladislav Saloun**. **Jan Neruda** and **Karel Capek** are also buried here, as are eminent Czech scientists and other intellectuals.

Around Vyšehrad

Leaving the park by the **Brick Gate** (*Cihelná*) will take you on to **Vratislavova** and then **Neklanova**, along which are some of Prague's finest examples of Cubist architecture. The Czechs were unique in developing this style from the principles first established in the Cubist paintings of Picasso and Braque. Using angular surfaces which 'deconstruct' solid objects into their constituent forms, a few such buildings were constructed before World War I brought such experimentation to a halt.

CUBIST LIVING

Tired of all that monumental Gothic and florid Baroque? Then what you need is a Cubist home. Most of the rebuilding in Josefov at the turn of the century was designed in Art Nouveau, but at the corner of Bílkova and Elišky krásnohorské there is an apartment block in Cubist style. The repeated geometrical shapes are reminiscent not only of paintings by Braque and Picasso, but also of the diamond sgraffito of the Schwarzenberg Palace in Hradčany. The effect is surprisingly pleasing, but Cubist architecture never really caught on. *See* pp. 86–7 for more examples in New Town.

The first example of the movement is at **Neklanova 30**: a block of apartments designed by **Josef Chochol** in 1913. Like all Czech Cubist architecture, the play of light and shade on the angular forms of the building help to create visual form and volume. At number 2 down the road, a Cubist façade presents itself to the street, designed by **Antonín Belada**. Around the corner on **Libušina** is a superb villa designed by Chochol: the **Kovařovocova vila**. Even its garden can be described as Cubist, with the railings set at a rakish angle. The balance and serenity of the design are marred only by the busy road outside.

EASTERN SUBURBS
Vinohrady *

The centre of Vinohrady – an attractive suburb to the east of New Town – is **Míru Square** (*Náměstí Míru*), surrounded by some splendid buildings and with an interesting market. Its central garden is overlooked by the twin towers of the **Church of St Ludmilla** (*sv. Ludmila*). Designed by Josef Mocker, the architect responsible for much of the Neo-Gothic façade of St Vitus' Cathedral, the church was built in 1893 with an attractive tympanum to the main portal sculpted by **Josef Myslbek**. Also on the square is the Art Nouveau **Vinohrady Theatre** – finished in 1907 – decorated with the figures of the four muses and some delightfully carved faces.

North of the Square is the **Riegrovy sady**, a large hillside park from which there are good views west over the city.

Žižkov

East of the the Riegrovy sady, Žižkov is dominated by its 1970s **television tower**. This is Prague's tallest and least popular building, erected to inhibit West German television transmission. Next to this offensive tower on Kubelíkova is a popular bar, the Akropolis, where one can sample **absinthe**, the heady

---

> **THREE VINOHRADY CHURCHES**
>
> The **Church of the Sacred Heart** (*Nejsvětější Srdce Páně*) on náměstí Jiřího z Poděbrad was built in 1928 by Josip Plečnik: its giant transparent clockface and bravura mixture of styles win it much admiration from contemporary architects. Nearby on U vodárny is Pavel Janák's 1930s **Hussite Church** (*Husův sbor*): the copper chalice on its tower is a symbol of the Hussite faith; notice, also, the plaque commemorating the church's part in the 1945 Prague Uprising. Josef Gočár's interwar **Church of St Wenceslas** (*sv. Václav*) on náměstí Svatopluka Cecha has a dramatically stepped roof and pencil tower.

Below: *Dvořák's gravestone is an elaborate tribute to the composer.*

BATTLE OF VITKOV

Jan Žižka was the colourful Hussite commander who led his peasant army to victory in July 1420 in the first battle of the **Hussite Wars**, the Battle of Vitkov. Žižka only had one eye, but he was a giant of a man who must have been a frightening sight, if his mace-wielding statue is anything to go by. He must also have possessed considerable charisma and been an excellent tactician. His ill-equipped force was vastly outnumbered by the imperial army of Emperor Sigismund, yet he won a decisive victory. Henceforth, Vitkov became known as Žižkov.

BLOWING-UP STALIN

David Cerný's metronome stands on the pedestal once occupied by the world's largest statue of Stalin. Blown up in 1962 by order of Moscow, the statue still lingers in Prague's memory, simply because it was universally hated. So prominent that it could be seen all over Prague, no one could get away from it: 30m (100ft) high, the statue portrayed Uncle Joe leading representative Czechs and Russians to the Promised Land of communism. **Otakar Svec**, the sculptor, killed himself before it was unveiled, and a year later, Khrushchev denounced Stalin.

---

liqueur which fired Van Gogh's insanity. Žižkov also boasts the largest equestrian statue in the world: 9m (30ft) high, it was erected in 1950 on Žižkov Hill to the north of the tower. Designed by **Bohumil Kafka**, it is a portrait of the military hero who gives his name to the suburb.

East of the television tower are Žižkov's two cemeteries. The first – the **Olšany** – contains the grave of **Jan Palach**, while the second – the New Jewish Cemetery – is where **Franz Kafka** is buried along with his family.

NORTHERN AND WESTERN SUBURBS
Letná Hill *

The park on Letná Hill – across from Josefov on the north bank of the river – was laid out in the 19th century, and in the communist era was the site of the annual May Day parades. There are fine views from the park, especially looking south along the river and its procession of bridges. The park's own most prominent feature is the giant red **metronome** designed by **David Cerný** and put in place in 1991 after the Velvet Revolution. Officially still a temporary structure, its symbolism – suggesting the transience of political regimes but the permanence of Prague – has yet to endear it to the city.

Right: *Cerný's giant metronome overlooks the Vltava.*

Also in the park is the **Hanavský Pavilion**, built in 1891 for the Prague Exhibition and moved here from its original site. A superb cast-iron structure, its Neo-Renaissance design makes it a close cousin of Art Nouveau.

National Technical Museum *

To the east of Letná, the National Technical Museum (*Národní technické muzeum*) on Kostelní 42 has a large collection of scientific and industrial artefacts. Its history of transportation section in the main hall comprises an enormous range of bicycles, trains, motorcycles, cars and aeroplanes – there is even a hot-air balloon suspended from the rafters. A collection of astronomical instruments includes some of Brahe's and Kepler's devices, and an exhibition devoted to clocks provides a cacophony of chimes on every hour. The basement – rather appropriately – has a large reconstruction of a coal mine (guided tours only). The museum is very popular with children.

Above: Elaborate Hanavský Pavilion staircase.

Museum of Modern Art and Výstaviště *

Thoroughly refurbished after the Velvet Revolution, the National Gallery's Museum of Modern Art (*Galerie moderního umění*) on Dukelských hrdinů inhabits the modernist Prague Trade Fairs Building, completed in 1928. Beyond it is the entrance to the complex of buildings constructed originally for the 1891 Prague Exhibition and which is now a popular funfair and entertainment centre. The chief building is the **Industrial Palace**, an iron and glass structure with a vertiginous open-air spiral staircase to its clock tower. The Art Nouveau **Lapidarium** (rebuilt in 1907) contains the National Gallery's collection of sculptures – rescued from the ravages of time and pollution from around Prague – and is especially worth viewing. There is also a planetarium, a diorama and gardens through which to wander.

MAY DAY MADNESS

The Sparta Stadium – Prague's main football ground – to the north of Letná was the venue for the annual May Day parades inaugurated by the communists after the end of World War II. Portrayed as a natural outpouring of communist solidarity, the parades were in fact the result of coercion and pressure. Thousands of citizens were forced to march past a red podium, from which their detested leaders smiled and waved. Ironically, it was the same stadium that witnessed the massive gathering of protesters calling for the national strike which brought down the government in 1989.

TUNNEL OF WATER

On the western perimeter of **Stromovka Park** an unobtrusive barn-like structure with an iron grille for a door is built into the hillside. Shaded by trees, it looks a strangely menacing place, but it is in fact the disused entrance to Emperor Rudolf II's water tunnel, constructed in 1584 to designs by the court painter Giuseppe Arcimboldo. The tunnel is over 1000m (3000ft) in length and is hewn from solid rock. Its purpose was to transfer water from the Vltava to the newly constructed lakes in the park further to the north.

Stromovka Park **

Contiguous with the Exhibition Grounds, Stromovka Park (more properly, the Royal Enclosure) was first created in the 13th century and opened to the public in 1804. It is one of the city's largest green areas, and perched atop an incline within the park is a lovely **Summer Palace** (*Místodržitelský letohrádek*). A medieval hunting lodge was the first structure on this site, built for the kings of Bohemia who hunted in the enclosure. The present Neo-Gothic building dates from 1805 and until 1918 it was the official residence of the Governor of Bohemia. It now houses the National Museum's collection of newspapers and periodicals and is closed to the public.

Elsewhere in the park there are various formal gardens and the remains of buildings long abandoned. The main path through the park crosses the Vltava, where there is a pleasant view from the bridge. By this point, the countryside begins to beckon and Prague city centre seems a long way off.

Troja ***

Troja Park begins across the river, within which is the splendid red and white **Troja Summer Palace** (*Trojský zámek*), built in the late 17th century by **Jean-Baptiste Mathey** for the aristocratic Sternberg family. This delightful building which is surely one of the most harmonious in Prague, sits amid formal French-style gardens (and also designed by Mathey) with a water fountain, maze, open-air theatre and two orangeries – behind the palace there are vine-clad terraced hills. The exterior of the palace is based on a Classical Italian model

Below: *Prague's parks offer a welcome retreat from the bustle of the city.*

Left: *The ornate staircase of Troja Palace is lined with mythical statuary.*

with two projecting wings and turreted belvederes. The most prominent feature is the magnificent double-staircase that climbs to the front door, its balustrading bristling with statues of gods and titans.

The sumptuously decorated interior of the palace took two decades to complete. The grand hall is one vast fresco depicting the glories of the Habsburg dynasty and the loyalty of the Sternberg family: Leopold I (1657–1705) is shown victorious over the Turks, his victims falling from the ceiling in the best traditions of *trompe-l'oeil*. There are also smaller chambers with murals of Chinese landscapes.

Zoo *

Prague Zoo (*Zoologická zahrada*) adjoins the western border of Troja Park, on slopes which overlook the scenic Vltava – a chair-lift can be taken to the highest parts of the zoo grounds. All the usual inmates are present, but the most famous animals in the zoo are the diminutive Przewalski horses, part of the zoo's successful breeding programme. Young children usually love zoos, of course, so it's a good place for parents to bear in mind when youngsters are tired of looking at Baroque architecture.

TROJAN PRAGUE

As wonderful as the Troja Summer Palace is, it's difficult to think of the original owner – **Count Wenceslas Adalbert** of Sternberg – as anything other than an incorrigible sycophant. He was desperate for the Habsburg monarch to stay in the palace if he ever came to hunt in the royal enclosure across the road. Hence the frescoes in the grand hall, which exhibit a stunning capacity for hero-worship. The name 'Troja' itself refers to Aeneas, the great Trojan hero who went on to found Rome, thus – in Sternberg's eyes – making Aeneas an ancestor of the Habsburgs.

8
Day Trips from Prague

The countryside around Prague has in some ways changed very little over the years: villages nestle in the folds of the forested hills, castles keep watch over the valleys and wistfully elegant spa towns still provide their healing waters. Many of these places of interest are accessible by coach excursion direct from Prague city centre and can be seen in a day or an afternoon. Alternatively, if you have your own transport these destinations are well signposted and make for a pleasant drive through the Bohemian countryside.

WHITE MOUNTAIN

On the western edge of Greater Prague – accessible by tram 22 – White Mountain (*Bílá hora*) is the site of the famous battle of the Thirty Years War, which decided the fate of Bohemia for the next three hundred years. In the 16th century, a royal hunting park and lodge were constructed on what was to be the battle site a century later. **Star** (*Hvězda*) hunting lodge is so called because it was built in the shape of a six-pointed star, its steeply sloping roof emphasizing every angle of the building. Constructed in 1556, it was restored in the 1950s and now houses a small museum dedicated to the writer **Alois Jirásek** and the painter **Mikoláš Aleš**. But the unusual building is itself the best exhibit. The sand-coloured walls of its simple and dignified exterior are nicely complemented by the large sweep of the red-tiled roof. Inside, it is beautifully decorated with elegant frescoes and stucco detailing.

DON'T MISS

*** Kutná Hora: historic medieval town.
** Karlovy Vary: large spa town amid forested hills.
** Karlstein Castle: fairytale castle overlooking river.
** Mariánské Lázně: small spa town with superb 19th-century architecture; forest walks.
** Křivoklát Castle: 13th-century fortress with Great Tower and prison dungeon.
* Lidice: museum and memorial to village destroyed in WW II.

Opposite: *The spa town of Karlovy Vary is surrounded by wooded hillsides.*

KARLSTEIN TREASURES

Karlstein Castle's Chapel of the Holy Cross – high in the Great Tower – was closed for restoration work throughout most of the 1980s. **Charles IV** kept his most precious relics and the imperial crown jewels in the beautiful Gothic chapel, behind more than a hundred wooden panels painted with the images of saints and angels. The chapel's low vaulting is entirely gilded and studded with hundreds of glass stars, a sun and a moon. Unfortunately, this top-secret imperial storehouse became damaged and worn by the huge number of visitors anxious to see it: access is now restricted.

Břevnov Monastery *

East of the park and just a few minutes' walk away is **Břevnov Monastery** (*Břevnovský klášter*). A Benedictine Abbey was founded here in the 10th century, but most of the present monastery – including the Baroque gateway and courtyard – are the work of **Christoph** and **Kilian Ignaz Dientzenhofer**. The outstanding building of the complex is the **Church of St Margaret**, which was built by Christoph Dientzenhofer in 1715. This is a *tour de force* of intersecting ovals, in its floor-plan and its exterior façade. A large building, it yet seems friendly and inviting, and is one of the most invigorating examples of Prague Baroque (interior access to the monastery is in groups by appointment, and there are guided tours on Saturdays and Sundays). The remains of the original 10th-century church can be seen in the crypt. The monastery meeting room – with its 18th-century frescoed ceiling – is also worth seeing.

BOHEMIAN CASTLES

Bohemia is famous for its magnificent castles, many of them perched impossibly on rocky crags and exuding medieval menace. Most are now little more than picturesque ruins amid splendid scenery, but there are a few better preserved examples which are very popular with tourists and visitors.

Karlstein **

Karlstein (*Karlštejn*) Castle is about 25km (16 miles) southwest of the city. In the best traditions of fairytale, it is set on a wooded promontory overlooking a river, and comprises a series of turreted towers and battlements within a crenellated wall that strides impressively down the hillside. It makes no difference that what you see is mostly 19th-century reconstruction and that little remains of the original 14th-century fortress built by Charles IV to house the crown jewels. It's great fun and children in particular, are pleased with the whole experience.

Konopiště *

Konopiště Castle is about 40km (25 miles) southeast of Prague. Set in extensive parkland on the site of a 13th-century fortress, the largely 19th-century structure still bears traces of Baroque construction, most particularly in its great gate sculpted by **Matthias Braun** in 1725. The castle has large collections of hunting trophies – mostly stuffed and mounted heads of animals – plus a good deal of arms, armour and porcelain. From 1897, Konopiště was **Archduke Ferdinand's** favourite retreat. Heir to the Austrian throne and married to a Czech, it was his assassination in Sarajevo in 1914 that sparked off World War I.

Above: *Karlstein Castle was founded originally in the 14th century by Charles IV to protect his royal treasures.*

SÁZAVA MONASTERY

A few kilometres away from Konopiště Castle, the beautiful Sázava River is overlooked by a great Benedictine monastery. Sázava was founded in the 11th century and was the only Bohemian monastery to use the Slavonic liturgy, making it an important source of **Slavonic texts**. The site also has two churches: an incomplete Gothic structure and a Baroque church made from the unfinished building. The monastery was dissolved in the 18th century, when it became a private residence. Some fine medieval frescoes still survive, and they can be seen on a guided tour of the buildings.

Above: *Magnificent views from one of the thermal baths at Karlovy Vary.*

Křivoklát **

Křivoklát Castle's similarity to Karlstein is due to **Josef Mocker**, who restored both castles in the 19th century. Much of the original 13th-century Přemyslid hunting lodge remains, as do signs of Charles IV's occupation (his daughter Margaret was born here). Křivoklát's dominant feature is its **Great Tower**, which is 42m (130ft) high. There is also a splendid Gothic chapel and a dungeon prison with a torture museum that includes the skeletons of prisoners discovered during restoration work.

THE SPA TOWNS
Karlovy Vary **

More famously known by its former name of Karlsbad, Karlovy Vary is 140km (85 miles) west of Prague, from where it can be reached by coach excursion and scheduled train or bus. Since the early 1500s the town has depended for its income on the healing properties of its 12 hot mineral springs. Its heyday was in the century before World War I, when the rich and the famous 'took the waters' in the elegant surroundings of the fashionable town: at one time or another **Beethoven**, **Karl Marx** and **Edward VII** all stayed here. Karlovy Vary's fortunes have faded since then, but it still provides cures to a vast public. In the summer months, there are delightfully bourgeois concerts, cultural events and racecourse meetings.

Much of the pleasure of Karlovy Vary consists in wandering among its *belle époque* hotels and villas, which drape themselves over the wooded hillsides upon which the town is built – see, especially, **Sadova ulice**.

TAKING THE WATERS

In 1370, Charles IV precipitated Karlovy Vary's transformation into an international spa by granting it the right to dispense medical treatments. The **spring water** – which bubbles up to the surface naturally in a range of temperatures from hot rocks deep beneath the earth – is used in all sorts of baths and massage treatments, prescribed to patients who undergo a strict regimen that can last weeks or months. The water is used to treat digestive disorders but it tastes quite nasty – sweetmeats are often eaten at the same time to mask the unappealing flavour.

The vast **Imperial Sanatorium** stands aloof on its hilltop site, watched by the bronze chamois at **Deer Leap** (*Jelení skok*) across the valley – accessible on foot and by funicular railway.

Kilian Ignaz Dientzenhofer's Church of Mary Magdalene (*sv. Maří Magdalény*) – built in 1736 – should on no account be missed; neither should the 19th-century **Russian Orthodox Church** with its gold onion domes. Churches of all denominations have been built here to serve the town's cosmopolitan population. The Corinthian-columned **Mill Colonnade** designed by **Josef Zítek** (architect of Prague's original National Theatre) is the town's 19th-century *pièce de résistance*.

Mariánské Lázně **

Formerly known as Marienbad, this spa town 170km (105 miles) west of Prague is smaller and younger than Karlovy Vary. The spa was founded in the early 19th century, although its 40 springs were known about as far back as the 1600s. Superbly located amid densely wooded hills, its late development has resulted in a delightful architectural uniformity: most buildings date from the second half of the 19th century. Pride of place goes to Mariánské Lázně's great cast-iron **Colonnade**, which was finished in 1889 – people taking the cure still stroll under its glass canopy. Like Karlovy Vary, it is fun just to wander through the town to admire the immaculate houses and wonder what it might be like to live in them. Most of Mariánské Lázně's villas and hotels have some sort of literary association: Goethe stayed at what is now the **City Museum** in 1823 and is commemorated in **Goethe**

THE GLASS SPA

Karlovy Vary is also famous for its **Moser glass**. Ludvik Moser opened a shop in the spa in 1857 to showcase the glassware he was producing in his decorating workshop. The spa's rich clients would prevail upon artists to engrave their portraits on glass, thus creating a lucrative market in engraved glassware. Moser's business grew steadily: the style and the cut of his glass were unsurpassed and his clients included several European courts. Moser went on to found his own glass-works and the Moser factory today still produces hand-blown glass for the luxury end of the market.

Below: *Beautiful Mariánské Lázně has many lovely buildings dating from the late 19th century.*

DESIGNING IN BONES

Sedlec – a northeastern suburb of Kutná Hora – contains a most unusual sight. A Gothic chapel in the graveyard to Sedlec's former monastery sits over the entrance to a subterranean ossuary, stuffed with human bones. The graveyard had become tremendously popular after it had been strewn with earth from **Golgotha**, so much so that by the 19th century something had to be done. A local artist named **František Rint** was asked to solve the problem. He formed the 40,000 complete skeletons into elaborate sculptures and even signed his name in bones, making him an early exponent of installation art.

Below: *The Collonade at Mariánské Lázně.*

Square (*Goethovo náměstí*). Franz Kafka spent the summer here in 1916, while other writers and musicians who took the waters include **Gogol, Ibsen, Kipling, Twain, Brückner, Wagner** and **Weber**.

The forested countryside around the town also provides some lovely walks.

KUTNA HORA ★★★

Established in the 13th century, this mining town 70km (45 miles) east of Prague, grew to become second only to the capital in wealth and importance. Until they gave out in the 16th century, the town's deposits of silver made the Bohemian king Europe's richest monarch. Much of the town's money was used to construct some remarkable buildings, the most important of which is the **Church of St Barbara** (*sv. Barbora*), which was begun in the late 14th century by **Peter Parler's** workshop. The church – dedicated to the patron saint of miners – has been described as one of the most beautiful in Europe. It rises majestically in an array of flying buttresses to three graceful tent-like spires, in an unsurpassed display of Bohemian Gothic wizardry. The unforgettable exterior is matched by a superb interior lit by intricately traced windows. It has a tremendous vaulted ceiling emblazoned with coats of arms and several superb Late Gothic wall murals depicting mining operations and saints. The magnificent Baroque organ case comprises a swirling multitude of gilded angels.

On the road lined with beautiful Baroque statuary that leads up to the cathedral, **Kilian Ignaz Dientzenhofer's** monumental **Ursuline convent** looks out across the valley. Kutná Hora's **Italian Court** (*Vlašský dvůr*) dates from the time of Václav II: now the town hall, it was the mint which for centuries produced the Prague Groschen, a silver coin that was at one time in circulation all over Europe. A guided tour takes tourists around Kutná Hora's unique Art Nouveau chapel. The town's **Mining Museum** allows visitors to explore part of the medieval workings which spread right under the village.

Other things to look out for as you wander through the delightful streets are the **Gothic fountain** and **plague column**, and the **Stone House,** the façade of which is carved with decorative relief work.

LIDICE *

The modern village of Lidice is situated approximately 19km (12 miles) northwest of Prague, but it should be noted that it is a destination which is not likely to be suitable for younger children. After the assassination of Reichsprotektor Reinhard Heydrich in May 1942, the old village of Lidice was chosen by the Nazis as an example and a warning. On 10 June, all the men of the village were shot and the women were taken to Ravensbrück concentration camp. The 89 children were taken to similar camps. The village was totally destroyed. The Nazis boasted that they would erase the name of Lidice from the map, but in fact quite the opposite occurred. Towns and villages all round the world changed their name to Lidice to preserve the memory of the people who died: thus did Lidice live on and good overcome evil.

The main street of the new village is called 10 Cervna 1942 (10 June 1942), the date of the atrocity. It leads to the various memorials that mark the location of the old village, which is now just a grass-covered field. There is a small, harrowing museum that includes original *SS* film footage of the burning village.

No matter what the weather or the season, Lidice is a disturbing place, but visitors may find there a little hope to take away with them.

Above: *The Church of St Barbara at Kutná Hora.*

TEREZIN

This fortress town is some 60km (37½ miles) northwest of Prague. Built in the 1780s by the Habsburgs, it was used by the **Nazis** as a transit camp for Jews from all over Czechoslovakia on their way to the concentration camps. Its informative museum traces the history of the Jewish ghetto, when Terezín was used for propaganda purposes as a kind of 'show camp' to convince the outside world – and international Jewry – that Jewish people had nothing to fear. Testimony from former inmates tells a completely different story. Terezín's official and hidden purposes are described in detail.

Prague at a Glance

BEST TIMES TO VISIT

Every season has its attraction and you may want to time your visit to Prague to coincide with a particular event, for instance the Prague Spring Music Festival (*Pražské jaro*), which begins on 12 May, or the Christmas festivities, which really start to liven up in early December with the setting up of festive market stalls in Old Town Square.

Prague enjoys a continental climate, which means that while summers can be stiflingly hot, the **winter** months from November to March are usually bitterly cold and the skies an unalluring leaden grey, which can give the city a forlorn look. On the other hand, snow enhances the beauty of the buildings and there can be no more magical place than Prague at Christmas. **Spring** is a delightful time to visit the city, when trees are starting to bud and the days are becoming warmer. **Summer** brings city life out of doors and attracts greater crowds, with the consequence that finding a room or a place to eat at this time can be problematic. Advance booking is strongly advised.

GETTING THERE

By air: The easiest and quickest way to travel to Prague is by plane. The city has good airline connections with many European and North American cities, although travellers from Australia, New Zealand and South Africa are not served directly and will need to travel via London. Direct flights from London operate about four times daily, and flight time is around 2hrs. The national carrier, Czech Airlines (CSA), also flies from Manchester to Prague three times a week.

By road: If you are bringing your own car to Prague, items you must take with you are a valid driving licence (an International Driving Licence is advisable, essential for visitors not from the EU, USA or Canada), vehicle registration card and an international insurance certificate (green card).

By rail: Prague has good rail connections with the rest of Europe – all the major capitals are linked by train. The main rail station in Prague is the Art Nouveau Hlavní nádraží on Wilsonova, not far from the National Museum at the top of Wenceslas Square.

GETTING AROUND

Many of Prague's most important sights are concentrated within quite a small central area, and the best way of getting your bearings is simply to explore on foot – in fact, Charles Bridge is accessible only to pedestrians. Comfortable flat shoes are best for walking along the cobbled streets. Watch out for the trams, which run in the centre of the road in both directions.

If you want to cross the city more quickly, or if the streets leading up to Prague Castle from Lesser Quarter Square prove too steep to negotiate comfortably, Prague's **public transport** system is cheap, efficient and reliable. It comprises a metro system as well as a network of trams and buses. Be aware that during the morning and evening rush hours, between 06:30 and 08:30 and 15:00 and 18:30, public transport gets very crowded, and you'll probably find yourself pushing and jostling with the rest of them!

Tickets and tourist passes: Tickets are uniform across the public transport system and must be bought before you make your journey. Tickets must always be stamped or punched in the machines supplied, otherwise they are invalid. Ticket inspectors do make periodic checks and levy hefty on-the-spot fines on travellers without a valid ticket, so don't be tempted to travel without one.

Single tickets (*jízdenky*) are available throughout the city from tobacconists (*tabák*), street kiosks, newsagents, hotels or some shops, or they may be bought from the orange machines at some bus and tram stops and inside metro stations (exact

Prague at a Glance

change is required). Under 10s travel free, and children between 10 and 16 years travel at half price.

If you want to avoid the problem of not having the right change for the single-journey ticket, or if you plan to use the public transport system extensively, then a multi-day tourist pass (*turistická siťová jízdenka*) is an excellent investment. These passes, available for periods of between one and five days, can be bought from tourist offices and offer unlimited travel on buses, trams and trains. They do not need to be validated in the machines, but you should sign and date the ticket before using it.

Metro: The metro system is extremely smooth and easy to use. Currently it has three lines, A, B and C, and there are plans for the construction of a fourth, though this is dependent on the availability of appropriate funds. Plans are also in hand to extend the network further out into the suburbs.

It's a good idea to purchase a metro map from the tourist office to help you plan your route. Maps are also on display in some of the larger metro stations, and there's a map of the metro network inside trains above each of the doors.

Metro entrances are signalled by a large letter 'M' against an inverted triangle, in green (line A), yellow (line B) or red (line C). Once you've passed the ticket barriers, take the escalator down to the train platforms – beware, as some escalators travel very fast. Large, easy-to-read signs indicating the direction (*Směr*) of trains are suspended from the ceiling; the name of the terminal station (*Stanice*) is shown, so consult your metro map to check which direction you want. Another overhead sign indicates all the stations along the metro line on which you are travelling; the station you are at is circled in white, and connections (*Přestup*) to the other lines are also clearly shown.

Doors open and close automatically. During the journey, a recorded message in Czech announces the next station. With a single ticket you can change between metro lines as many times as you like within one hour, but once you leave the

underground system your ticket becomes invalid and you must stamp another one for subsequent journeys. Once you have arrived at your stop, follow the exit (*Výstup*) sign to find your way out of the metro system.

Trams and buses: You use the same single tickets for the trams as for the metro and bus networks. Once aboard the tram, you must validate your ticket in one of the small brown machines that you'll see attached to metal poles; insert your ticket in the black slotted lever and pull the lever towards you. Tickets are valid for one journey only.

Tram timetables are posted at tram stops. The stop at which you are standing is underlined, and all the stations below it are where the tram is going next. As with the metro, doors open and close automatically and a recorded announcement in Czech precedes each stop.

Travelling by tram is an excellent, and at times exhilarating, way of getting

PRAGUE	J	F	M	A	M	J	J	A	S	O	N	D
MAX TEMP. °C	0	1	7	12	18	21	22	22	18	12	5	1
MIN TEMP. °C	-5	-4	-1	3	8	11	13	13	9	5	1	-3
MAX TEMP. °F	32	34	45	54	64	70	72	72	64	54	41	34
MIN TEMP. °F	23	25	30	37	46	52	55	55	48	41	34	27
HOURS OF SUN DAILY	2	2.5	5	6	8	8.5	9	8	6	4	2	1
RAINFALL mm	18	18	18	27	48	54	68	55	31	33	20	21
RAINFALL in	0.7	0.7	0.7	1.1	1.9	2.1	2.7	2.2	1.2	1.3	0.8	0.8
DAYS OF RAINFALL	13	11	10	11	13	12	13	12	10	13	12	13

Prague at a Glance

around; some hurtle round corners at unsettling speeds. The tram service is frequent and reliable, and reaches into all parts of the city, offering cheap sightseeing possibilities. At night, a limited number of trams runs every 40 minutes from around midnight to 05:00.

You're unlikely to use the city's bus system, which covers the more outlying suburbs. Buses are noisy and dirty, and for the most part are kept well out of Prague centre. If you do use the bus, the procedure for buying and validating tickets applies as for trams and the underground.

Taxi: Taxi drivers have acquired something of a reputation for tourist exploitation which may or may not be universally deserved; be that as it may, you're advised to use taxis with caution. A minimum charge applies as soon as you step into the taxi; after that there is a legally fixed rate per kilometre. If you suspect you've been overcharged, ask for a receipt (*potrzení*), which must be given by law if requested.

Car rental: Considering Prague's extensive public transport system, as well as its confusing web of one-way streets and its shortage of parking spaces, driving around the city is not really a viable option. If you do want

to hire a car, perhaps to use for day trips from Prague, one of the cheapest companies is **Esucar** at Husitská 58, Prague 3, tel: (02) 27 88 88. Other more expensive but better known agencies include: **Avis**, Krásnohorské 9, Prague 1, tel: (02) 231 55 15; Airport Ruzyně, Prague 6, tel: 316 67 39, **Budget** at the Hotel Intercontinental on Pařížská, tel: (02) 248 81 11, or **Europcar**, Pařížská 26, tel: (02) 24 81 12 90.

WHERE TO STAY

There is no shortage of places to stay in Prague, but finding something to suit your budget poses a little more of a problem. Since 1989, many new hotels have sprung up, mostly to accommodate the luxury or business markets, while older hotels have been refurbished or brought up to international standards with greater or lesser degrees of success. Prague's best hotels in the best central locations are inevitably the most expensive, and you'll need to make reservations before you travel. A number of new hotels with good facilities are situated in the suburbs, though their location is usually inconvenient for sightseeing. There are very few cheap or moderately priced hotels in the vicinity of Old Town, Prague Castle or the Lesser Quarter.

Hotels by no means offer the only accommodation option in Prague. Rooms in **private homes** or **self-catering apartments** offer sometimes significantly cheaper alternatives to hotel rooms; a room in a family home is less impersonal and is an excellent way of making Czech friends. For more information, *see* **Travel Tips** on p. 122. If you are dialling from outside Prague, the telephone area code is (02).

LUXURY

Don Giovanni, Vinohradská, Prague 3, tel: 67 03 67 03, fax: 67 03 67 04. A new international 400-room hotel a little out of the centre of Prague (nearest metro stop: line A, Zelivského). Predominantly aimed at business visitors; facilities include restaurant, pub and café bar, fitness club and conference rooms,

Hotel International, Koulova 15, Prague 6, tel: 24 39 31 11, fax: 311 83 00 or 24 31 06 16. The hotel has a wine restaurant and there are regular entertainment programmes, including folklore evenings and wine-tastings.

Paříž, U Obecního domu 1, Prague 1, tel: 24 22 21 51, fax: 24 22 54 75. A glorious Art Nouveau building that was declared a historic monument in 1984. Rooms are disappointingly bland compared to the beautiful craftsmanship on display in

Prague at a Glance

the hotel's public spaces, but they are comfortable and well maintained. Live music and traditional jazz concerts are regular features in the Café de Paris.

Pod Věží, Mostecká 2, Prague 1, tel: 53 37 10/53 18 95, fax: 53 18 59. A new hotel in an extremely good location beneath the Lesser Quarter Bridge Tower. There's also a restaurant that specializes in Czech, Jewish and international cuisine.

Prague Hilton Atrium, Pobřežní 1, Prague 8, tel: 24 84 11 11, fax: 24 81 18 96. A vast 11-storey atrium hotel which looks more like an office block than a place to stay. There are 788 rooms and suites, with all the facilities you'd expect from an international establishment, including four restaurants, a fitness centre and two indoor tennis courts. Situated 30 min from Ruzyně airport.

Savoy, Keplerova 6, Prague 1, tel: 24 30 24 30, fax: 24 30 21 28. Under the management of Vienna International Hotels and Restaurants. Superbly located just a few steps from Prague Castle; every Sunday there's a jazz brunch in the hotel's acclaimed restaurant.

MID-RANGE

Adria, Václavské náměstí 26, Prague 1, tel: 24 21 65 43, fax: 24 21 92 74. Good central location on Wenceslas

Square, though bear in mind that this area turns into the city's disco and red light district at night.

Alta Praha, Ortenovo náměstí 22, Prague 7, tel: 800 252-9, fax: 66 71 20 11. A new hotel with 87 well-appointed rooms, a restaurant and other first-class facilities.

Atlantic, Na Poříčí 9, Prague 1, tel: 24 81 10 84, fax: 24 81 23 78. Right in the heart of Prague, this hotel has 60 rooms as well as two restaurants and a winter garden.

Parkhotel Praha, Veletržní 20, Prague 7, tel: 24 31 23 76, fax: 24 31 61 80. Large, somewhat impersonal hotel located on the road from the airport 15 min from the city centre; conference facilities for business visitors.

BUDGET

Pension Unitas, Bartolomějská, tel: 232 77 00. Former prison cells once used by the secret police, converted into two-, three- and four-bed accommodation for visitors on a shoestring. Václav Havel was an involuntary resident here.

Kafka, Cimburkova 24, Prague 3, tel: 27 31 01, fax: 27 29 84. Clean, simple and comfortable.

Pension City, Belgická 10, Prague 2, Vinohrady, tel: 351 96 22, fax: 691 09 77. Clean and colourful.

U krále Jiřího, Liliova 10, Prague 1, Staré Město, tel: 24 22 20 13, fax: 24 22

19 83. Charming little pension, with Prague's only Irish pub.

YOUTH HOSTELS

Domov Mládež, Dykova 20, Prague 10, tel: 25 06 88; fax: 25 14 29.

Slavoj-Vesico Hostel, V Náklích 1, Prague 4, tel/fax: 46 00 70.

WHERE TO EAT

The dearth of good, cheap hotels is more than outweighed by the number of excellent, reasonably-priced eating establishments to be found all over Prague. The choice is varied, too, from cheap cafés and pizzerias to one of the most expensive French restaurants in the Czech Republic. In between is a whole host of unpretentious places offering a range of cuisines, not just Czech but Chinese, Greek, Lebanese and more.

Prices are cheap by Western standards, and you can expect to pay no more than around 500 Kč for a three-course meal with wine in a good establishment. Be aware that a 23% tax, which should normally be included in the menu, is occasionally added to the total bill.

Vegetarians will not have as hard a time of it as they might have expected, given the Czech predilection for meat. Pizzerias and cafés with meat-free snacks

Prague at a Glance

abound, while two excellent restaurants for a more expensive meal out are U Cedru and La Provence (see below).

The places listed below give an impression of what's available, but do bear in mind that restaurants in Prague close down, or change management, with surprising regularity. For the latest and best recommendations consult the 'Dining Out' section of The Prague Post, which gives reliable and respected ratings. Credit cards are now widely accepted, at least at the more upmarket restaurants, but it's advisable to check beforehand.

LUXURY

Avalon Circle Line, Malostranské náměstí 12, Prague 1, tel: 53 03 08/53 02 76. The speciality here is succulent shellfish; reservations are advisable.

Fakhreldine, Klimentská 48, Prague 1, tel: 232 79 70. An excellent Lebanese restaurant, which has received much acclaim since it first opened in 1994. Reservations advisable.

U Laury, Nerudova 10, Prague 1, tel: 55 10 83. The menu changes daily at this cosy wine cellar restaurant in the Lesser Quarter. There's also a good selection of Moravian wines.

Lobkovická Vinárna, Vlašská 17, Prague 1, tel: 53 01 85. Imaginative fish and

meat dishes and attentive service; reservations advisable.

U Malířů, (The Painter's), Maltézské náměstí 11, Prague 1, tel: 24 51 02 69. This is the country's most expensive eating establishment, but also its only genuine gastronomic French restaurant. Ingredients are brought in from France twice a week for the French chef to create his *pièces de résistance*, served in suitably elegant surroundings. Reservations essential.

U Modré Kachničky (The Blue Duck), Nobovidská 6, Prague 1, tel: 24 51 02 17. Just off Maltese Square in the Lesser Quarter, this is an intimate, romantic and beautifully decorated place that specializes in meat and game; reservations are essential for dinner.

Parnas, Smetanovo nábřeží 2 (at Národní), Prague 1, tel: 24 22 76 14. Regarded as one of the city's best restaurants; popular Sunday brunch from 11:00 to 15:00; reservations recommended.

La Provence, Stupartská 9, Prague 1, tel: 232 48 01. Delightfully furnished surroundings and freshly prepared food in generous portions evoke the atmosphere of southern France, even if it is snowing outside. Vegetarians can eat well here, and the service is prompt yet friendly. There's a nightclub and tapas bar

upstairs, so it can get very noisy; reservations not necessary, but advisable.

MID-RANGE

Caffe-Ristorante Italia, Nerudova 17, Prague 1, tel: 53 03 86. There's nothing remarkable about this bright, clean and efficient café-restaurant, but its pasta dishes are very acceptable and it makes a convenient stop if you're in need of refreshment after visiting the Castle.

Ça Va Restaurant, Pařížská 20, Prague 1, tel: 24 81 10 10. In Josefov, this restaurant offers a wide range of dishes prepared by its French chef. There's also a reasonable selection of French wines.

U Cedru (The Cedar Tree), Na Hutích 13, tel: 312 29 74. Fresh pink tablecloths and starched white napkins don't immediately conjure up images of the Orient, but the food quickly dispels any doubts. Lebanese cuisine is the speciality in this small, friendly restaurant; spicy falafels, stuffed vine leaves, smoked aubergine dip, tabbouleh and other (mostly) vegetarian starters are more than enough to satisfy hungry diners, and you probably won't be able to manage a main course. The cardamom-brewed Arabic coffee is a good restorative. Reservations recommended in the evening.

Prague at a Glance

Cerberus Bar and Restaurant, Soukenická 19, Prague 1, tel: 231 09 85. Cocktails and healthy, light food prepared using fresh herbs.

Zlatý Býk (The Golden Bull), Mělnická 13, Prague 5, tel: 53 75 44. Specialities are as diverse as quails' eggs or pheasant to down-to-earth mushroom soup; the quality of the ingredients is consistently good.

BUDGET

Bella Napoli, V jámě 8, Prague 1, off Vodičkova, tel: 24 22 73 15. Italian delicacies include tortellini Gorgonzola, excellent pizza and a good choice of wines.

U Knihomola International Bookstore, Mánesova 79, Prague 2, tel: 627 77 67. Downstairs from the bookshop is a café offering light, French-style snacks and wine in a literary atmosphere.

The Globe Bookstore and Coffeehouse, Janovského 14, Prague 7, tel: 66 71 26 10. A favoured haunt of the expatriate American community, this small, lively, occasionally smoke-filled café offers a good range of mostly vegetarian soups, filled rolls and cakes, including delicious chocolate brownies. There's an equally small bookshop attached, with a rather eclectic collection of new and second-hand books.

Sate, Pohořelec 152/3, Prague 1, tel: 53 21 13. Spicy Indonesian food, including sate (skewered pork served with a peanut sauce).

U zeleného Caje (Green Tea), Nerudova 19, tel: 53 26 83. Tiny but very popular vegetarian café serving herbal teas and light snacks. You'll need to get there very early, as there are only four tables.

PUBS AND BEER HALLS

Pubs and beer halls (*pivnice*) are all over Prague. Some are real 'locals' which don't really cater for visitors, while others go all out for the tourist trade: if in doubt stick to the centre of the city. As well as the excellent Czech ales and beers, many establishments serve hearty Czech food in very sizeable portions – the quality of which may be variable but the quantity can always be guaranteed. Don't wait to be seated, but select your table and wait to be served. You may be joined by others if the place is crowded. Most bars and beer halls open from 10:00 in the morning until around 22:00 or 23:00 at night.

U Fleků, Křemencova 11, tel: 29 32 46. Founded in medieval times, this large, popular *pivnice* is famous for the strong dark beer brewed on the premises.

U Kalicha, Na bojišti, 12–14, tel: 29 07 01. Virtually all the food and drink and certainly all the decor is on a *Good Soldier Svejk* theme. Popular with tourists, less so with the locals.

U Zlatého tygra, Husova 17, tel: 24 22 90 20. Crowded pub with literary connections and clientèle.

Jo's Bar, Malostranské náměstí 7. Well-situated bar serving predominantly Mexican food to an appreciative American crowd. Popular on Sundays.

SHOPPING

The range and quality of goods available in Prague shops has improved considerably since the transition from the old, centralized economy under communist rule to a market-based economy. A growing number of leading Western multinationals have been making their presence felt since 1989, and the country as a whole is being gradually introduced to a consumer-oriented culture. One consequence of this is that it has become increasingly difficult to pick up genuine bargains as prices rise to match Western levels, though there are bargains to be had, especially in goods such as glass, ceramics, CDs, books and wooden toys.

Most of the city's best shops are concentrated round the centre, especially

Prague at a Glance

round Old Town Square, Pařížská, on and around Celetná, and around Wenceslas Square. As many of these areas are pedestrianized, strolling around looking in shop windows can be a pleasurable activity, though you'll inevitably be contending with crowds of other like-minded window-shoppers.

For indoor shopping, the **Vinohradský Pavilon** at Vinohradská 50 is an exclusive commercial centre that occupies the site of a former fruit and vegetable market. Over 60 brand-name boutiques selling everything from clothes, sportswear and household goods to electronic equipment are clustered under the Neo-Renaissance roof. The centre is open seven days a week, 09:30–21:00 Monday to Saturday, 12:00–18:00 Sunday.

Markets are good places to browse round and watch some good-natured haggling, though the quality of the goods on offer is not always very high. The largest and oldest market is held at **Holešovice** in converted abbatoir buildings at Bubenské nábřeží 306. Everything is here, from fruit, vegetables and poultry to electronic gadgets. In the city centre, there is a popular open-air market in **Havelská** that specializes in fruit, vegetables and wooden toys.

Undoubtedly the best time for markets is in the weeks running up to Christmas, when Old Town Square is taken over by wooden stalls selling everything from hot spiced wine to candles, jewellery, ceramics, puppets and handmade Czech crafts.

Charles Bridge is covered in street stalls throughout the year, and in summer these are supplemented by others around Old Town Square, the Castle and Na příkopě. Some are run by young Czech artisans finding an outlet for their designer jewellery, Prague watercolours, wooden toys and unusual artefacts, but many offer mass-produced 'Russian' army memorabilia, cheap watches or other tacky tourist merchandise.

Glass, crystal and porcelain: Bohemian glassware and porcelain are of exceptionally high quality and are highly prized throughout the world. Designs range from traditional to contemporary, from chunky vases to exquisite slim-stemmed wine glasses. The best glass and china is produced by **Moser** works in Karlovy Vary and on sale in the **Bohemia Moser** shop at Na příkopě 12. Shops will pack your purchases securely and can arrange carriage to your home, at a price of course.

Interesting specialist glassware shops include:

Bohemia Crystal, Mostecká 13, Prague 1.
Crystalex, Malé náměstí 6, Prague 1.
Crystalex, Bohemia Moser, Staré náměstí 27, Prague 1.
Dana Bohemia Glass, Národní 43, Prague 1.
Jafa, Maiselova 15, Prague 1. Crystal Gallery, Štěpánská 51, Prague 1.
Mappin and Webb, Karlova 27/144, Prague 1. Also jewellery, clocks, gifts.

Musical instruments and CDs: Musical instruments are beautifully made and less expensive than in the West. Sheet music is also cheaper. Classical music buffs will be impressed by both the range of CDs available and the advantageous prices. One of the best places to buy classical music is **Matouš**, which occupies the ground floor of the Goltz-Kinský Palace in Old Town Square. The choice of CDs is extensive and you can listen to the music through headphones before making your purchase. Other good music shops can be found all over the city, especially along Pařížská, Národní, Na příkopě and Jungmannovo (off Wenceslas Square).

Dům Hudebních Nástrojů, Jungmannovo náměstí 17, Prague 1.
Hudební Nástroje Berdych, Nekázanka 20, Prague 1. Largo, Náprstkovo 10, Prague 1.

Prague at a Glance

Praha Music Center, Revoluční 14, Prague 1.

Bookstores: Even if you don't read Czech, it's a treat to browse round any of Prague's second-hand bookshops (*antikvariát*) as they are so attractively laid out, and there's often a good selection of old prints and posters. Catering for the sizeable expatriate community are a number of English- and foreign-language bookstores, two of which – the Globe and U Knihomola (Bookworm) – also have cafés.

Big Ben Bookshop, Rybná 2, Prague 1.

International Bookstore Praha, corner of 17. listopadu and Pařížská, Prague 1; large selection of English-language books.

Melantrich, Na příkopě 3, Prague 1. Other branches on Wenceslas Square, Old Town Square and elsewhere.

The Globe, Janovského 14, Prague 7. Excellent store with adjacent café.

U Knihomola International Bookstore, Mánesova 79, Prague 2. Generally a selection of classier coffee-table books and the like.

Antikvariát Galerie Můstek, 28 Rijna, Nové Město; metro Mustek, contains one of the largest selections of old maps, prints and paintings in Prague.

Czech design and traditional crafts:
Original one-off designs by young and coming Czech artists make fabulous and surprisingly affordable gifts. The Ivana Follová Art and Fashion Gallery has three shops in Prague, all stocked with original handmade clothes, jewellery, accessories, ceramics and prints, some outrageous, all unique.

Ivana Follová Art and Fashion Gallery, Rytířská 27, Prague 1 (near the Estates Theatre); Maiselova 21, Prague 1; Ve Smečkách 23, Prague 1 (off Wenceslas Square, catering for men).

For more traditional Czech souvenirs, there is a wide variety of handcrafted items available, including wooden toys, beautifully painted Easter eggs, ceramics and figurines in folk dress. One of the best shops is Krasná Jizba (The Beautiful Room), with a good selection of folk art.

Krasná Jizba, Národní 36, Prague 1; Melantrichova 17, Prague 1; Husova 12, Prague 1.

Department stores:
Department stores are not quite the equivalent of what most Westerners would understand by the term. The range of goods is sometimes rather eclectic and the quality variable, though Kotva in Republic Square has

a good range of smoked meats in its basement food hall. K Mart is a popular, cheap, American-owned store that sells almost everything from food to electrical goods.

Bílá Labuť, Na poříčí 23, Prague 1; Václavské náměstí 59, Prague 1. Fur hats and good groceries.

K Mart, Národní 26, Prague 1. Everything from groceries to hi-fi equipment.

Krone, Václavské náměstí 21, Prague 1. Good grocery.

Kotva, Náměstí Republiky 8, Prague 1. Large store with food hall on lower floor.

Baťa, Václavské náměstí 6, Prague 1. Well respected shoe store.

Dětský Dům, Na příkopě 15, Prague 1. Caters for children. Excellent cheap clothes and shoes.

Ikea–DBK, Budějovická 64, Prague 4. The well-known Swedish furniture and homeware chain.

TOURS AND EXCURSIONS

Although Prague is so compact and well served by public transport, it might be a good idea to get your bearings by taking a city sightseeing tour. There are several available, some of which combine coach and boat trips. Some tours are arranged by theme, for instance a walking tour around the city's Old Town treasures, or a bus tour of Prague's famous residences.

Prague at a Glance

Organized trips are also available to many of the excursion destinations described on pp. 104–11 of this book. Many of them will include guided multilingual commentary, lunch and/or (depending on the destination) free museum entrance, wine-tastings, a sampling of mineral spring waters or a glass of Becherovka liqueur. Tours generally start from náměstí Republiky or Wenceslas Square.

If you prefer you can organize your excursions before you leave for Prague by contacting the Czech Tourist Centre. Or try any of the local operators – prices are competitive so it's worth shopping around. In general the cheaper tours are offered by Prague Information Service, the more expensive by Cedok. The American Express and Thomas Cook offices both offer extensive travel services besides sightseeing tours in Prague and the Czech Republic.

Specialist cycling tours through the most interesting and scenic areas of the Czech Republic are organized by MIKE, a travel agency based in Mělník. Itineraries vary in degree of difficulty and accommodation is arranged along the route. For information, contact your Czech Tourist Centre or write to **MIKE** at Ostruhová 62, CZ-276 01 Mělník, Czech Republic,

UK:
Czech Tourist Centre Ltd, 178 Finchley Road, Hampstead, London NW3 6BP, tel: (0171) 794 3263/4, fax: (0171) 794 3265.
Cedok, 49 Southwark St, London SE1 1RU, tel: (0171) 378 6009.

Prague:
American Express, Václavské náměstí 56, tel: (02) 24 21 99 92, (02) 24 03 23 08, fax: (02) 24 22 77 08.
Cedok, Na příkopě 18, 111 35 Prague 1, tel: 24 19 71 11, Pařížská 6, tel: (02) 231 69 78, fax: (02) 232 17 28; a variety of tours in the Czech Republic ranging between castles, river cruises and sightseeing trips in and around Prague.
Fischer Reisen, Celetná 9, tel: (02) 231 77 27, (02) 232 18 09, fax: (02) 232 90 62, (02) 232 39 32; Prague sightseeing tours.
Prague Information Service, Na příkopě 20, tel: (02) 54 44 44.
Premiant City Tour, Mostecká 21, tel:/fax: (02) 53 36 84.
Thomas Cook, Václavské náměstí 47, tel: (02) 24 22 95 37, fax: (02) 26 56 95.
VIP Tours, tel:/fax: (02) 232 77 83; sightseeing in minibus or limousine.
Welcome Touristic Praha, Klimentská 52, tel: (02) 231 46 61, (02) 231 46 55, or ask at your hotel reception.

USEFUL CONTACTS

Airport, Central Information Service, tel: (02) 36 77 60, (02) 20 11 11 11.
American Center for Culture and Commerce, Hybernská 7a, tel: (02) 24 23 10 85; exhibitions, newspapers, library and business reference service.
Bohemia Ticket International, Salvatorská 6, tel: (02) 24 22 78 32, fax: (02) 24 81 03 68; Na příkopě 16, tel: (02) 24 21 50 31; Karlova 8, tel: (02) 24 22 76 51 – you can buy your concert tickets in advance, though it's more expensive than going direct to the box office.
British Council, Národní 10, tel: (02) 24 91 21 79, window gallery for temporary exhibitions, library and resources centre and satellite Sky TV news.
Customs Office Headquarters, tel: (02) 24 06 11 11.
Czech Railways Travel Agency (České Dráhy – Cestovní Kancelař), Hybernská 5, tel: (02) 24 21 98 05, fax: (02) 24 22 36 00.
French Institute, Štěpánská 35, tel: (02) 24 21 66 30, screenings of classic French films as well as a popular café.
Lost Credit Card Line, tel: (02) 236 66 88 or (02) 24 72 53 53.
Lost and Found, Bolzanova 5, tel: (02) 24 22 61 33.

Travel Tips

Tourist Information

Since 1989, there has been a proliferation of private tourist agencies. Professional standards and range of services vary, but there is no shortage to choose from. The former state-owned **Cedok** now operates as a private agency and still offers a broad range of tourist services, from travel and accommodation, currency exchange and car rental to guided tours, books, leaflets and maps. The **Prague Information Service** (PIS) has an efficiently run office in Na příkopě in the city centre and provides maps, listings and advice as well as offering guided sightseeing tours. Many agencies employ English-speaking staff, but a working knowledge of German should also come in handy.

American Express, Václavské náměstí 56, tel: (02) 24 21 99 92, fax: (02) 24 22 77 08. Offers a wide range of travel services. **Cedok**, Na příkopě 18, tel: (02) 24 19 71 11, fax: (02) 232 16 56. Travel tickets, car rental, exchange office.

Pařížská 6, tel: (02) 231 69 78, fax: (02) 232 17 28. Tours in the Czech Republic, castles and chateaux, river cruises, sightseeing trips. Rytířská 16, tel: (02) 26 27 14, (02) 26 63 10, fax: (02) 26 60 86. Trips through Bohemia and abroad, exchange facilities.

Czech Centre of Tourism, Národní 37, tel: (02) 24 21 14 58. Tourist information and brochures.

Pragotur, U Obecního domu 2, tel: (02) 232 511 28.

Prague Information Service, Na příkopě 20, tel: (02) 54 44 44; Staroměstské náměstí 22 (inside the Old Town Hall), tel: (02) 24 21 28 45.

Thomas Cook, Václavské náměstí 47, tel: (02) 24 22 95 37. Business travel, tourist programmes, currency exchange.

For general information contact the Czech Centre, 30 Kensington Palace Gardens, London W8 4QY, tel: (0171) 243 7981.

Embassies and Consulates

Canada: Mickiewiczova 6, Prague 6, tel: (02) 24 31 11 08, fax: (02) 24 31 02 94.

Republic of South Africa: Ruská 65, Prague 10, tel: (02) 67 31 11 14, fax: (02) 67 31 13 95.

UK: Thunovská 14, Prague 1, tel: (02) 24 51 04 39, fax: (02) 24 51 13 14.

USA: Tržiště 15, Prague 1, tel: (02) 24 51 08 47, fax: (02) 24 51 10 01.

Entry Requirements

To enter the Czech Republic, visitors must have a passport (valid for at least six months beyond the return date). Visitors currently not requiring a visa are those from the EU, USA and Canada; other nationals are strongly advised to check the latest situation at their nearest Czech consulate (see above for addresses).

Customs

Residents of EU countries are allowed to bring into the Czech Republic personal effects for use during their visit in the following quantities: 2 litres of wine, 1 litre of spirits, 250 cigarettes (or the equivalent in cigars or tobacco), and for hunting purposes, 1000 shotgun pellets or 50 rifle bullets. These quantities can also be exported duty free, in addition to gifts up to the value of 1000 Kčs and any goods purchased with foreign currency in a Tuzex shop. You should always keep receipts as proof of purchase. Information from General Customs Head Office, Václavské náměstí 57, tel: 24 06 11 11.

Health Requirements

Your hotel should be able to put you in touch with the local doctor or, in an emergency, call the ambulance (dial **155**). Health care provision is shared between the state and private sector. Emergency medical attention is provided free of charge for foreign visitors from countries with reciprocal health agreements with the Czech Republic, otherwise all non-emergency treatment must be paid for on the spot. You should therefore take out adequate insurance. Be sure to obtain a receipt for your insurance claim.

Alternatively, there is a 24-hour emergency service for foreign visitors at the Diplomatic Health Centre (Nemocnice Na Homolce), Roentgenova 2, tel: (02) 52 60 40.

Some **pharmacies** (lékárna) stay open after regular business hours. A 24-hour service is offered by the pharmacy at Na příkopě 7, tel: (02) 24 21 02 29.

USEFUL PHRASES			
ENGLISH	**CZECH**	**ENGLISH**	**CZECH**
airport	letiště	**visa**	vizum
bill/check	účet	**petrol**	benzin
bus	autobus	**pharmacy**	lékárna
car	auto	**police**	policie
castle	hrad	**post office**	pošta
church	kostel	**railway**	
closed	zavřeno	**station**	nádraži
entrance	vchod	**stamp**	známka
excuse me	promiňte	**street**	ulice
exit	východ	**ticket**	jízdenka,
guide	průvodce		vstupenka
hospital	nemocnice	**thank you**	děkuji
how much?	kolik to stojí?	**today**	dnes
I don't under-		**tomorrow**	zitra
stand	nerozumím	**tour**	jízda
I understand	rozumím	**train**	vlak
information	informace	**tram**	tramvaj
lavatory	toalety	**when**	kdy
lost property	ztráty a	**who**	kdo
	nálezy	**where**	kam
open	otevřeno	**yes/no**	ano/ne
passport	pas	**yesterday**	včera

Emergency **dental** treatment is provided at Vladislavova 22, tel: (02) 24 22 76 63. The **First Aid Centre** (Služba prbní pomoci) at Palackého 5, tel: (02) 24 22 25 21, can give advice and basic remedies. If you are prescribed certain medication, it is advisable to bring an adequate supply with you, as equivalents may be difficult or impossible to obtain in Prague.

Getting There

By air: The easiest and quickest way to travel to Prague is by plane. The city has good airline connections with many European and North American cities, although travellers from Australia, New Zealand and South Africa are not served directly and will need to travel via London. Direct flights from London operate about four times daily, and flight time is around 2hrs.

The cheapest standard fare is an Apex return, which must be reserved at least 14 days in advance. The national carrier, Czech Airlines (CSA), also flies from Manchester to Prague three times a week and offers a wide range of promotional deals. Discounted flights to Prague are widely advertised in the UK Sunday newspapers, but bear in mind that in peak season flights are booked up several weeks in advance.

By road: If you are bringing your own car to Prague, items you must take with you are a valid driving licence (an International Driving Licence is advisable, essential for visitors not from the EU, USA or Canada), vehicle registration card and an international insurance certificate (green card). You also need to carry replacement bulbs, a hazard warning triangle and a first-aid kit, and your car should bear a national identity sticker. Note that the minimum age for driving in the Czech Republic is 21.

By rail: Prague has very good rail connections with the rest of Europe – all the major capitals are linked by train. The main rail station in Prague is the Art Nouveau Hlavní nádraží on Wilsonova, not far from the National Museum at the top of Wenceslas Square.

What to Pack

It's advisable to bring something warm such as a sweater or jacket and a raincoat as Prague experiences a great deal of rain throughout the year. From May to August the days are long and hot, with the warmest temperatures between June and July. Cool cotton clothes are essential for comfortable sightseeing, though an umbrella is useful to ward off sudden summer showers. Flat, comfortable shoes are best for negotiating Prague's steep hills and cobbled streets. The wettest months are from October to November, when temperatures also begin to drop. Snow usually starts to fall in November or December, and continues through January and February; during these months it can get bitterly cold.

Money Matters

Currency: The unit of currency in the Czech Republic is the crown (*koruna*), abbreviated Kč. The crown is divided into 100 hellers (h). Czech banknotes come in denominations of 20, 50, 100, 200, 500, 1000, 2000 and 5000 Kč; coins as 10h, 20h, 50h, and 1, 2, 5, 10, 20 and 50 Kč. It is illegal to import or export Czech crowns; surplus notes can be converted back into western currency at the airport (keep your exchange receipts).

Currency Exchange: Money can be changed at most banks, hotels and currency exchange offices. Banks offer generally the best commission, though the queues are often long and slow-moving. There are hundreds of small, privately run bureaux de change all over the city. Be warned: many charge large commissions, or if they don't their rate of exchange is disadvantageous. In their favour, some exchange bureaux are open 24 hours and you won't have to wait around. **Never** change money on the black market; not only is this illegal, but you run the

very real risk of being cheated.

Travellers' Cheques: The safest way of carrying money is in the form of travellers' cheques – Thomas Cook and American Express are the best known. Cheques must first be changed into crowns, as they are not accepted as currency by shops or restaurants.

Credit Cards: Credit cards such as Visa, MasterCard (Access) and American Express are becoming a widely accepted means of payment in Prague, and you'll almost certainly be able to use plastic in the more expensive hotels, shops and restaurants.

Tipping: Tipping is not generally required but is greatly appreciated should you decide that the service has been particularly attentive.

VAT: Value added tax (sales tax) of either 5 or 23% is normally included in the total cost of the item sold; food is exempt from VAT. There is no tax-free shopping in Prague.

Accommodation

Although accommodation has become much easier to

CONVERSION CHART		
FROM	**TO**	**MULTIPLY BY**
Millimetres	Inches	0.0394
Metres	Yards	1.0936
Metres	Feet	3.281
Kilometres	Miles	0.6214
Kilometres square	Square miles	0.386
Hectares	Acres	2.471
Litres	Pints	1.760
Kilograms	Pounds	2.205
Tonnes	Tons	0.984
To convert Celsius to Fahrenheit: x 9 ÷ 5 + 32		

find in Prague, it is advisable to book in advance if you're travelling during the high season (from Easter until September) or over Christmas. Hotels are clean and most have been modernized to meet acceptable standards. Self-catering apartments or rooms in private homes offer a convenient and cheaper alternative to hotel accommodation. For information contact: In the UK: **Czech Travel Ltd, Essex**, tel: (01245) 328647. **TK Travel**, London, tel: (0181) 699 8065. In Prague: **AVE Travel Agency**, tel: (02) 24 22 32 26, fax: 24 22 34 63. **CKM**, tel: (02) 231 12 35. **Pragotour**, tel: (02) 231 12 35.

Eating Out

It is possible to find somewhere to eat at almost any time of day, at least between the hours of 10:00 and 02:00. From simple stand-up fast-food stands (*bufet*) and cafés (*kavárna*) to upmarket wine cellars (*vinárna*) or restaurants (*restaurace*), the choice is much wider than you might expect. Traditional Czech food may be sampled in beer halls (*pivnice*), though the emphasis here is usually on downing litres of the local brew. There are a number of well-known hamburger chains for the inveterate fast-food addict.

Transport

Air: Prague's international airport, Situated 15km (9

PUBLIC HOLIDAYS
1 January • New Year's Day **March/April** • Good Friday and Easter Monday **1 May** • May Day **8 May**• Liberation Day **5 July** • Sts Cyril and Methodius Day **6 July** • Anniversary of Jan Hus' death **28 October** • Independence Day **24–26 December** • Christmas

miles) northwest of the city centre, Ruzyně currently has 24-hour exchange facilities, car rental, a duty-free shop, restaurant, post office and left-luggage office. It is linked to the centre by a regular CSA bus service; buses leave usually every hour from outside the arrivals building. Taxis are readily available.
Road: A motorway toll coupon (*dálniční známka*) costing 400 Kčs per car (valid for one calendar year) is essential for travel within the Czech Republic. It can be bought at Czech border crossings on arrival.
Road conditions: Outside the main towns roads are relatively free of traffic and well signposted, but driving conditions in winter can be treacherous.
Driving regulations: In urban areas, the speed limit is 60 kph (37 mph), on dual and single carriageways 90 kph (56 mph), and on motorways 110 kph (68 mph).

Children under 12 are not allowed to travel in front.
Drink and driving do not mix – the permissible blood alcohol level for drivers is 0.00 per ml, and penalties are severe for any infringement.
Buses: The city's main bus terminal is Florenc, located on the eastern edge of New Town. It serves all international routes as well as long-distance journeys within the Czech Republic. The station has timetable information posted, but most staff speak German or Russian as their second language and not English.
Rail: Express trains (*Rychlíl*) travel to major towns and may require a supplement in addition to the price of a normal ticket. Slow passenger trains (*Osobnýs*) are very slow indeed and usually stop at every station. Tickets for all trains can be purchased in advance.

Business Hours

Museums, galleries, castles and other tourist sites are usually open from Tuesday to Sunday 09:00 or 10:00–17:00 or 18:00, closed Mondays. Some remain open throughout the year, but others close in winter, so check with the tourist office before you visit.
Most **banks** are open Monday to Friday 08:00–17:00, and are usually closed over lunch for an hour between 12:00 and 14:00. The Komerční banka at Na příkopě 42 is

open until 19:00 weekdays and 09:00–14:00 Saturdays. **Post offices** are open Monday to Friday 08:00–18:00, Saturday 08:00–12:00. **Food shops** are open from as early as 06:00 until 18:00 Monday to Friday, and 07:00–12:00 Saturday; other shops generally open 09:00–18:00 Monday to Friday, 09:00–12:00 Saturday. Many shops in the centre of Prague, especially those catering to tourists, stay open until 19:00 or later, and some are open on Sunday as well. Many **pubs and restaurants** close at 22:00 or 23:00.

Time Difference

Prague is one hour ahead of GMT and uses the 24-hour clock.

Communications

The general post office (*Hlavní pošta*) at Jindřišská 14, not far from Wenceslas Square, is open 24 hours; for information, tel: (02) 24 22 85 88. Parcels and valuable letters may be posted during the day from the general post office, and, after 20:00, from the post office at Hybernská 13, tel: (02) 24 21 97 15. **Faxes** can also be sent from the main post office. A fax to the UK will cost about 40 Kčs per minute.

Electricity

Standard continental 220 volts AC. Most European appliances should work with a two-pin round plug adaptor.

Weights and Measures

The Czech Republic uses the metric system.

Health Precautions

No inoculations are required for travel to the Czech Republic. **Ambulance transport**, tel: (02) 37 33 33. **Diplomatic Health Centre for Foreigners**, Na Homolce, Roentgenova 2, tel: (02) 52 60 40. Doctors speak English and German. **Emergency Medical Aid** (English), tel: (02) 29 93 81. **Emergency Dental Treatment**, Vladislavova 22, tel: (02) 24 22 76 63.

Personal Safety

Compared with other cities in Europe and North America, Prague has a low crime rate and assaults against tourists are rare. The biggest security problem comes from pickpockets, who are rife in summer in the main tourist sights and on the trams and metro. Take sensible precautions such as carrying with you only as much money as you need, leave passport and tickets in your hotel safe, and note down credit card and travellers' cheque numbers. Women travelling alone should avoid Wenceslas Square and the area around the main railway station at night.

Emergencies

If you have been robbed go to the police, as your insurance company will require a police report. Police headquarters is in Old Town at Bartolomějská 6, tel: (02) 24 13 11 11.

Police, tel: 158.
Ambulance, tel: 155.
Fire, tel: 150.
Other useful numbers:
Lost Credit Card Line, tel: (02) 236 66 88 or (02) 24 72 53 53.
Traffic accidents, tel: (02) 77 34 55.

Language

The national language is Czech, and any attempt at speaking it will be greatly appreciated. If you find the combination of vowels too daunting, a knowledge of German will be very helpful, while English is now increasingly spoken or at least understood among the younger generation. For further information see p. 23.

GOOD READING

• Bruce Chatwin, *Utz* (1989). Compelling tale of an obsessive collector set in post-war Prague.
• Slavenka Drakulić, *How We Survived Communism and Even Laughed* (1992). Feminist perspective of life under the communist regime.
• Timothy Garton Ash, *The People: The Revolution of 89* (1990). Eye-witness account of an extraordinary year in Europe.
• Jaroslav Hašek, *The Good Soldier Svejk and his Fortunes in the World War*. Picaresque tale of the Czech Republic's most infamous fictional character.
• Václav Havel, *Living in Truth* (1989). Celebrates the playwright-President's fight for freedom of thought.

INDEX